A Lifetime of Words

A Lifetime of Words

Jan Seale

LITERARY PRESS
LAMAR UNIVERSITY

ISBN:9781942956808
Library of Congress Control Number: 2020940597
Cover design and author photo by Erren Seale

Lamar University Literary Press
Beaumont, Texas

*for all who find the art of writing
an irresistible attraction*

Recent Prose from Lamar University Literary Press

Robert Bonazzi, *Awakened by Surprise*
David Bowles, *Border Lore: Folktales and Legends of South Texas*
Chris Carmona, Rob Johnson, & Chuck Taylor, *The Beatest State in the Union*
Kevin K. Casey, *Four-Peace*
Terry Dalrymple, *Love Stories (Sort of)*
Gerald Duff, *Legends of Lost Man Marsh*
Britt Haraway, *Early Men*
Michael Howarth, *Fair Weather Ninjas*
Gretchen Johnson, *The Joy of Deception*
Christopher Linforth, *When You Find Us We Will Be Gone*
Tom Mack & Andrew Geyer, *A Shared Voice*
Moumin Quazi, *Migratory Words*
Harold Raley, *Lost River Anthology*
Harold Raley, *Louisiana Rogue*
Jim Sanderson, *Trashy Behavior*
Jan Seale, *Appearances*
Jan Seale, *Ordinary Charms*
Melvin Sterne, *The Number You Have Reached*
Melvin Sterne, *Redemption*
Melvin Sterne, *The Shoeshine Boy*
John Wegner, *Love Is Not a Dirty Word*
Robert Wexelblatt, *The Artist Wears Rough Clothing*

CONTENTS

Introduction

I have spent a lifetime enjoying words. Luckily, words have also been the tools of my profession: writing, teaching, and public speaking. It is very seldom that one can have in one's tool box the necessary implements that will define, refine, expand, contract, amend and deliver a product. In this case, we writers are very lucky, with an infinite supply of utensils, in infinite reordering, to work toward the product, which is, of course, meaning.

This miscellany grew out of my need to collect in one place a representative number of speeches and articles which had escaped collection in one of my other books. Some are presentations given orally but never recorded anywhere except in my personal files. Others are articles which have seen the light of day in magazines and journals, while a few have appeared in one or another of books authored by me but seemed worth repeating for their subjects celebrating written words and stories. As I worked on some cohesion, a theme emerged: a lifetime of working with, using, and just plain loving language. I have included here those works which might in some way speak to that obsession.

Who might be an audience for such a collection? A various one. There would be those acquaintances politely curious about what direction their longtime writer-friend had headed off in. In addition, I am hopeful that young writers and teachers will find usefulness in the experiences and thoughts expressed here.

"Part One: Words Choose Us" contains reasons for delving into the writing arts, particularly a rationale for writing poetry. It also contains an interview which spells out my activities as a teacher of writing and storytelling over the years.

"Part Two: Creations and Re-creations" makes a case, through examples of short works, for broadly interpreting our material, using craft until we find the right vehicle to carry our messages. I had in mind in particular when preparing this section novice writers struggling to shape their material.

"Part Three: Practice Makes More Practice" deals with a number of my interests as reflected in articles, essays, and presentations over the years. It offers some observations on title-making, self-editing, marketing, and exercising creative joy.

Some of the writing here has been edited slightly for clarity, length, or to avoid duplication. I have purposely left some dated quaintness in these essays, for example, my opening volley in the first issue of *riverSedge* in which I rail against difficult poetry. (I still believe some of this today.) I did expunge a passage where I was encouraging newbie poets not to be stingy with their *stamps and envelopes, with return envelopes.*

"Part Four: Journaling" offers a discussion of the kinds of journals I've kept through the years: a general/writing journal, one for dreams, another for gratitude lists, and four for observations about my four grandsons. I find the journals particularly useful for writing starters and for filling in the details. In addition, journaling is a great way to talk to one's self, thereby saving many friendships and preserving the good will of relatives.

"Part Five: Looking at the Light" contains a little history of the light-footed poet laureate phenomenon in Texas, as well as a presentation I made many times throughout Texas in the 1990s as part of the Scholars program of the Texas Council on the Humanities. The subject of that one, preserving and treasuring the stories of families, is one ever dear to me. And it is so especially since I am now one of the elders of whom I speak.

"Part Six: Poems on Writing" samples my take on writing poems over the years. It may come across as a little acerbic; most of the poems here are not illustrative of the great themes of poetry. They comment on writer's block, accepting criticism, and bringing poetry to an indifferent world. It is my lot to deal with difficulties in the publishing world as I do some other life stumbling blocks, that is, with humor, albeit irony and sarcasm. In the end, though, as the last poems here suggest, there is the thrill in participating in the magical mystery of poetry.

I am a record keeper, a chronicler, possibly learned early because I have a mediocre memory. Just for the record, I offer the following statistics on my lifetime of being in love with words, and on the secondary profession of talking about words, that is, teaching writing.

Although I wrote my first poem early on, at about six, and continued to write through my growing years, my written notes regarding the profession start in 1967 (when I *had* a six-year-old) and proceed to the present 2020, where I hope to make a few more entries before the dark.

As for the writing itself, I count 412 poems published, 167 articles and essays, and 42 short stories. These were often first published in magazines and journals and then sometimes included in my books where appropriate. The books themselves number ten of poetry, five of nonfiction, two of short stories, and ten for children. At times I've had the privilege of being a spectator to my work. Nine dramatic works have been performed on stage, sometimes with multiple performances. That's the good news.

The coda to this cheerful enumeration is that yes, I have in my proud possession a figure of 1205 poetry rejections and 365 article, essay, and story rejections. I hope these figures will encourage young writers to take heart and keep on keeping on.

As for the teaching, I taught some kind of writing classes for 36 years, including junior high, high school, university, and adult education. In addition to these regular classes, by my count I have presented my writing on 55 university campuses, made 77 artist-in-the-classroom visits to elementary and high schools—some of these weeklong, had 25 educational consulting jobs, and conducted 45 workshops. As if that wasn't fun enough, I've been privileged to do readings and give speeches on 126 occasions in such venues as museums and bookstores, as well as to be invited to furnish the program at 80 club meetings over the years. Thirty-one literary contests have been subjected to my opinion.

I sit back and look at this record, wondering what it all means. You may be wondering as well. If you are young, these figures may forecast your own considerable output over half a century. If you are a seasoned writer reading this description of numbers, I hope you are appreciating your own unique record that your day-by-day labor has produced. Spend a while giving yourself credit for the entirely worthy but time-expensive task of sharing your life, your conjuring, your words with others. As an aside, I hope this book will in particular encourage my generation of Texas writers—a great bunch—to share the evolution and maturation of their writing lives.

11

I would be remiss if I failed to thank all those who have helped make my lifetime of words happen. There were fine editors and publishers, discerning fellow and sister writers, inspiring teachers, and attentive students. There were arts managers, program chairpersons, and club members. There were patient loyal friends who took time to read a bedtime chapter or a few pages of poetry and later tell me their reactions. There were family members who indulged my solitary hours and preoccupation with writing projects. And there were those who spoke so encouragingly that I took these expressions as permission to go on writing and teaching and speaking, feeling fortunate indeed to have the words of the English language to transport my thoughts and imaginings.

Part One: Words Choose Us

Meanings receive their dignity from words.
~Pascal

Why I Write

When our sons were growing up, we maintained for them a special place in the house dubbed the make-it drawer. In it resided all sorts of recycled thingamajigs such as burnt-out light bulbs, cardboard cylinders, ribbons, broken watches, and melted crayons. I think I even remember at one time a beautiful old iridescent beetle and some monarch butterfly wings.

The boys went to this drawer when they wanted something to do. Once, when a boy was pasting a ribbon on a board, he said apologetically to anyone around who would listen, "I'm just doing this to keep from going crazy."

Writing is like delving into the make-it drawer and finding something to do to keep from going crazy. But wait—there are lots of perfectly sane folks around who don't write and who don't go crazy. So what is it, I ask myself, especially on difficult writing days, that keeps me at this solitary, uncertain-of-the-outcome task?

A circular answer is that I keep writing because I have kept on doing what I began doing early in life. Call it perpetual motion or a low threshold for change. I started writing when I was six, alone and ill in bed months at a time. There were no playmates, no TV, only easy tools like books and paper and pencils. I availed myself of them—probably to keep from going crazy.

By the time I was well enough to go to school, I found words had become my best friends. They were available and were the vehicles for taking captive the things and people and situations around me that were endlessly interesting.

I have always been a little drunk on sheer existence. Nothing, but nothing is boring unless it is willed to be—not the entire physical world, not one's life experiences, not the unseen spirit of dreams and revelations.

But one can participate in "the rapture of being alive," (Joseph Campbell's label) and still not be a writer. It is only those who have the urge to share the rapture who turn to the strange business of writing.

I had a fear of flying until I was 35 years old. When I finally climbed on a plane, I went from panic to elation. What a fantastic view—tidal pools and wandering roads and crop patchworks and old volcanoes! And what did I want to do with all this panoramic glory? Turn to my friend or a startled stranger and say, "Look at this!"

So I think for me writing is this primal inability to keep something to myself. I see it: it thrills or appalls, entrances or teases. What to do with this idea that has come my way? I turn to my seatmate—hopefully a sympathetic or at least curious reader—and declare it.

Most writers have overall philosophical reasons for writing, and then specific practical ones at any given time. In the middle of the night, I may reach for my journal when I can't sleep. I will write and write and write about my everyday circumstances. I may rant, rave, celebrate, explore. Or I will make a list of tomorrow's to-do's which have chosen to invade my rest. These writings are purely personal, although later I may go back to them and find something I can use in a writing project.

And from time to time I write on specific assignment, such as writing a trail guide for our local nature center or writing a speech for a presentation to a church group, club, or business association.

Sometimes I'll come across a writer in my writing classes who worries that their writing day job—say, writing grant proposals—has somehow blunted their talent for the poems and stories they aspire to write. A wise friend articulated the answer I give in these cases: "All writing is good for all other writing." I don't worry that writing about the chachalaca or the guamuchil tree in a semi-technical way will disturb my sonnet writing or flash fiction.

I write faster and better when I have specific goals. These may be from the outside, such as calls for poems or stories on a particular subject (I love the classifieds in *Poets & Writers*), competitions, or requests from editors. If none of these are calling me, I have learned through the years to make up my own projects, with structure and deadlines. Hopefully, when I follow through, these writings will reach a wider public than my file drawer.

I was very fortunate to have a father who loved words, who quoted poetry and wrote some himself, as well as over 400 newspaper columns. His father was also a word lover, with less than a high school education but who maintained an entire room in his house just for his books.

Then I was lucky enough to marry a fellow artist, a musician and composer who understood that I needed peace and quiet to write. The three sons who came along seem to have inherited the creative itch possessing their father and me. As well as being directed to the make-it drawer on boring days, they grew up viewing what their parents were doing in words and musical notes as perfectly natural.

I comment on them as part of my reasons for writing because whatever their care exacted from me as their mother (and for many years I spent much more time at the kitchen stove and in the car pool than at my writing desk), I count it my good luck that they were by nature sympathetic to "Mother's poems." Moreover, they supplied me with both whimsical and serious material for my writing.

Few who live long enough escape periods of preoccupation with crisis of one kind or another. My life has been no different. Money, illness, accidents, difficult relationships, sorrow, care giving. And for the writer there is rejection, wrongheadedness, impatience, the too-fast brain, the slowed-down brain. Why we rise from these obstacles, brush ourselves off and keep writing, may indicate, at the last of all our rational reasons for writing, a simple obsession.

I like to believe that a big reason for writing is getting to places of knowing and understanding, and then converting these into wisdom. We writers are such committees! We require the discipline of writing to call ourselves to order, to still ourselves enough to think. And in doing so, we may manage to ferret out the artificial and untrue, that is, the "unthoughtful."

Most writers probably come to writing in the first place bearing this objective: to know their own minds and hearts better. It's a compelling goal; otherwise, writing—at least for a public—is too hard: solitary, mentally and emotionally demanding, chancy.

Marshall Cook, a Wisconsin writer, puts it this way, "When you see writing as a way of thinking and discovering as well as a means of expressing your thoughts and feelings for others to share, writing becomes an indispensable part of your life, less destination than journey, less something you do than something you are."

Moving about in the randomness of human existence, we find our material from this common soil. We look, we feel, we exult, we abhor. We determine to make sense of our existence, to give utterance to what strikes us as significant, to share the bliss and the pain. And maybe simply to play along the way.

I talked by phone to one son this morning. He had a day off from his regular business of owning and running a commercial photography studio. I asked, "What are you planning to do with your day?"

He replied, "Oh, I'm going to work—but on my own stuff." The stuff is more photography, but of a different sort. I thought how he was in a good place artistically; with the luxury of some time, he enjoys his art, not distinguishing altogether between "work" and "play."

That is how it is sometimes in writing. I'm writing because I have this urge to play. And it's always a game of chance. I pit myself against an idea that has occurred to me. Can I come even close to winning it over to the page? Can I draw new elements, like cards or dominoes, from the pile? How is it dictating its hand to me? At the end of a writing period, I may be happy with my score, or smile wanly and opine, Maybe another day. As Isak Dinesen put it, "I write a little every day, without hope and without despair."

I feel the cynicism of our times acutely. There is a sense in creeping nihilism that anyone who hasn't given up hope for humanity is naïve. It's trendy to be analytical, begrudging, and despairing. The atmosphere begs violence and contentiousness. As Colette wrote, "There are moments, when you're aware of how cruel and sad the world can be and have to choose between optimism and pessimism."

Writers have to take a stance on where they are in this climate. I think I'm meant, perhaps only by default, to write mostly in celebration of the world that endures in spite of evil. It may be a calling, something like a mission beyond why I write for personal reasons.

I've thought a lot about Robert Louis Stevenson's observation for children: "The world is so full of a number of things/I think we should all be as happy as kings." A number of kings in the world are presently not all that happy, but we understand the metaphor and can embrace at least the first part of the quote. The world is still full of a number of marvelous things.

Our writing affords us a privilege that few of the millions on earth have. I am daily grateful to have been chosen for this work. Some of why I write will forever remain a mystery to me. It's one of those mysteries that keep me moving ahead, peering down the path. What, I ask, might be there waiting for me to write about tomorrow?

Artist Statement

We are, all of us, part of a storytelling and story-receiving species. To enhance our lives, whether we are writers or readers of writing, we can all be open to discovery. Julia Cameron, a writing teacher, observed, "The capacity for delight is the gift of paying attention." Delight is the payback for close observation.

Animal behaviorists tell us that in a given monkey family, twenty percent of them are sent to the top of the canopy in the forest to act as lookouts for food and for the safety of the group, to call down the news. I always want to be one of those designated story-telling monkeys.

What can we find new in our lives each day and thus celebrate? I make a game of finding something different in my backyard or in a park near my house where I walk. The other day I got close enough to see the throat contours change on a mockingbird as it sang. What a marvel!

Sometimes my dreams leave me in awe of that whole mysterious process. The poet William Blake said, "Everything that lives is holy. / Life delights in Life." Do you delight in life?

There is a story in everything and everybody. Do we give the gift of listening as well as of telling? Do we understand that one's story may be more important than any schedule or budget or report? Occasionally, when I'm tempted to want to "pass" on another's story, I try to remember a line from the Desiderata: "Listen to the boring; they have their story too." Listening to a story you've heard over and over, and one that doesn't immediately draw you in, may be a sacrament, a gift to the person who needs so badly to repeat it. The paradox is that if we listen closely enough, and with our hearts, we find that even in the most ordinary, familiar story, there will be something for us as well.

We need to keep our hearts and minds open to the possibility of deeper meanings. If I already know everything I'm going to say in a poem, I probably won't write it. I want to experience what the writing will tell me.

Remaining human in a time-share world allows our interpretation of the events in our lives, our recall, to change if need be, but always to ripen, to enlarge, to be subject to the way we are growing as human beings.

Introduction

Lately I have been thinking about how our poems choose us. Forever before, a poem does not exist, and then, some day when we least expect it, or conversely, are fervently entreating it, there it is.

We can attend workshops, study the great poetry masters, graduate from writing programs, write with fair ease a villanelle or a pantoum, and yet, and yet, the poems we write are, in a sense, the peculiar ones we are destined to write.

Poem-making chose me early on, before I knew how to get the words on paper. Recalling that time, I think of myself holding my hand to one ear, rocking back and forth, repeating the line that had startled itself into my young brain, and coaxing the next thought out of hiding—always in meter and rhyme.

Like all good mysteries, we come to a place where we are stumped by the origin and the urgency of the poems we write. Of course, we can trace our subjects by our genes, inheritance, experiences, emotions, and our close observations of the world and its stories around us.

But why does a certain idea tap us on the shoulder, clear its throat, positively insist that we pay it attention? When we do, one thing leads to another. More ideas come forward. Do they fit with the original one? Or do they demand their own poems? At some point, we simply stretch out our hands to receive our unique parcel, the thrill and the work of poetry.

If we're lucky, the mystery travels through us and renews itself in the alert listener or reader, the enjoyer, if you will—as that person receives the poem. And if we poets would be generous practitioners of our art, we will often position ourselves as the benevolent hearers of others' poems.

But it doesn't do any good for a poet to envy another poet's gift. That is time wasted. We will always owe a great debt to the masters, our poetic forebears. And we may learn from our contemporary favorites, enjoying them to the fullest, even thrilling to them, but we must not believe for one minute that the exact same talent can be ours. Those admired poets have their unique gifts. We need to become, and remain, their affirming audience, not their jealous critics or adoring sycophants.

It's good for a poet's soul to be generous to other poets, to lift them to the light so that poets and their audiences everywhere can find each other, taking deep pleasure and solace in the art. It is not good to spend time yearning to write poems that are not in us, that are not our givens. Better to spend that time striving to receive our subjects, along with their treatments, the ways they desire to be born and live in the world of thought. Better to surrender to the mysterious claims on our own minds and souls.

Regardless of our age or experience, all of us have plenty to write about. The young have yet to put in the hours of living, but they have their energy and enthusiasm to bolster what experience they do have. Their elders have a vast set of years to draw on, as much as their concentration and life circumstances will allow.

Reflecting on the poems in this volume, I have little explanation for many here which chose me as their amanuensis over a thirty-year period. By that I mean that they seem at this vantage whole, or done—irrevocable and inevitable.

And now, with this second edition comes a sampling of a dozen new poems from the emerging decade under the heading "South by Southwest." Of course I've written many more poems on other subjects in the last few years, but these, which I first thought of labeling "Location, Location" bunched themselves, hefty enough to insist on harmonizing with the earlier themed sections. They bring the poems in the volume back to the landing pad of the first section, "Crossing to Either Side." Yes, after 40 years, I am still here, deep in the feet of Texas.

Some may conclude that with the importance I have given in my writing to my homeland—really almost an outpost, just a few miles from Mexico—that I should be branded a 'regional writer.' It seems to me that that old limiting label has about played itself out, but if not, I gladly submit, observing that all writers really are 'regional', if we're paying attention to what's going on around us, if we address our surrounds, and if we would accept the givens of our lives, one of which is our habitat.

When *The Wonder Is* first appeared, a wise friend opined that I had not dated each poem, to make more chronological sense of the journey to my readers and show my progression as a poet. I understood his point.

I know generally in which period of my life a poem was written, and many indicate that by their subject matter or by when they were first published, but there were years when poem-making and living the outer life ran pell-mell over each other. With a family, a teaching career, and a gregarious nature, I often struggled to find a lone place in my days for writing, much less to record the date when I pronounced a poem finished. Some general periods are obvious, for example, when parenting or academics were in the ascendancy; likewise, the women's movement, war (take your pick which one), and environmental awareness.

Am I embarrassed by any of my poems written twenty or thirty years ago? Okay, yes, a few that are published, and some hidden carefully in my study in a folder marked "early poems." Still, here in my eighth decade, I am surprised that I am more satisfied than not with poems written so long ago. Then, I was who I was; the poems were what they were. It may be that, after all, the center holds. Our poems keep insisting we claim them because, again, they are the ones we are uniquely meant to write.

These days I feel wiser and more cautious, in certain ways tougher and in others more tender. The young radicalized passionate poem-maker has become more introspective and moderate, more accepting. She is sometimes alarmed and certainly more grasping as the future shrinks. She is still often confused but always amazed by life, and ever willing still to embrace it.

There's plenty of wonder to go around.

Preface to Poems

Sometimes writing is solace, sometimes an alleluia for the pleasure of getting to exist.

I write to set my thinking in order, to entertain myself, to see if I can offer a little piece of the puzzle about the human condition, which often turns out to be seriously humorous!

Writing is a calling, just like any other profession. Writers are called to observe and feel keenly, and then to articulate their findings to whoever might want to listen. Writers are here to write, to fill that peculiar slot. If one writes, knowing that she is doing what she is supposed to be doing, that is the important thing. Then publication becomes the fine by-product that it should be.

I'm a curiosity seeker, with stories and poems about the things and people that attract me to think about them, often by their oddness. I have poems on stuffed wolves, wax churches, fire-eaters, and monster birds. In stories, my subjects are often lovable bumblers or innocents or exotics.

Besides this ever-loving need to write—and sometimes in conjunction with, my passions run toward saving the wildlife of South Texas, helping older people record their life stories, and encouraging women to know and appreciate their contributions. And I'm a family woman: I'll do whatever it takes to strengthen my clan.

Essay from *Ordinary Charms*, Lamar University Literary Press, 2017

Frightening Words

Some folks like big cars, fancy clothes, long vacations. I like words. My license plate says WORDS and I'm not letting go of this customized designation even if I do have to pay extra for it.

I've been interested in words all my life. I have been accused of going to the zoo and getting more interested in the names of the animals than in the animals themselves. I can't help it if I tour the enclosures repeating "double-wattled cassowary" just for the pleasure of rolling it off the tongue.

People like me are called writers, and they know a good set of tools when they see it. But just as a tool can saw a board with precision, it can also cut off a finger. In other words, writing is a two-edged sword. We have logophobia, fear of words, and at the same time graphomania, the urge to write.

There are words I have never made peace with in their meanings such as "vetted" and "ubiquitous," such as "inimical" and "eponymous," words I have to look up every time just to be sure I'm correct in my usage.

I think I have conquered the difference in "continual" and "continuous" but the mnemonic device I use is way too elaborate: "continual" has just two letters in the final syllable, meaning frequent, while "continuous" has three, meaning constant.

Then there are those words that (or is it which?) refuse to lie quietly in my brain waiting until I am ready to write them with correct spellings, words like "maneuver," "siege," "silhouette," "camouflage," "souvenir," "khaki" and "niece." They always look wrong to me, even when they're right. And, as an English teacher in another life, I hate to admit that a simple pair like "shirt" and "skirt" keep me inordinately alert when I write or read them. I am further flummoxed by these two because now a garment has been invented called a "skort"—which is a pair of shorts covered by a skirt front.

I think it's perfectly all right to use a word in a poem that I am unshakable on as to meaning, but I break out in a cold sweat when I'm reading a poem to an audience and suddenly don't remember how the word is pronounced. Is the mountain flower "LOO-pine" or "loo-PEEN," the bird "gos-hawk" or "gosh-awk"? And what to do with those awkward consonants in the middle of words like "unkempt," "kiln," and "comptroller"? I have carefully looked them up, even several times, but malevolently forget the results of my research.

And then there are words that one knows the meaning of, knows how to pronounce, but still approaches with dread because they threaten to do unnatural things in the mouth. These include "sepulchral," "Cro-Magnon," "arctic," "anonymity," "graminivorous," and "Banff (National Park)." The all-time winner in this category is "vulnerable," which my Ph.D. friend pronounces over and over in speeches as "vunerable."

A subcategory of dreaded words is filled with those lately sprouting from our techno-tendency to stop hyphenating compound expressions. So we have "minibio" which might stump us as "mi-NEE-bee-o" unless we remember that it's describing a small resume, or "miniseries," which wants to read "min-ISS-er-eez," something we'll not be watching week after week on TV.

Certain words I'm afraid to use because, though they're perfectly legitimate, they sound lewd. They are the near-twins of words that should be avoided in polite company. I will probably abstain from the good word "slitless."

I heard of a teacher who used the principle of near-miss suggestive words to get the attention of her teenage students the first day. She simply stated a rule: "I don't want anyone masticating in this room." Another teacher, a choir teacher tired and longing for the close-of-day bell, had finally verbally wrestled her noisy tenor section into listening to her reminder. In a moment of confusion, and perhaps in a pure Freudian slip, she told them, "Absolutely do not forget the sexual rehearsal tomorrow morning."

Then there's "titivate," a word meaning to make a decorative addition to, definitely within blushing range. So are certain legal words. I myself never want to be called a "testatrix," nor any of my male loved ones the "testator." For that matter, neither do I aspire to be a "regina." Let's leave that one to the queen.

Connotations of ugliness churn up when we consider the names for milk products. Aurally ugly are modern terms such as "yogurt," "whey," "sour cream," and "whipping cream." A few have fallen into disuse, and so much for the better, such as "curds" (Remember Little Miss Muffet who sat on a tuffet eating her curds and whey?), as well as "clabber," a disused word today because it names soured unpasteurized milk, something we seldom run across. And suddenly, "blue john" has tripped through my synapses as I hear my mother saying it as she peers down into some thin skim milk possibly gone bad.

The world is swimming in words and sometimes their uses are so ludicrous that we can only sit back and laugh. A local podiatrist's office has a sign in the waiting room that says, "Our mission: to provide the highest quality of foot care in a comforting, passionate, and understanding environment." A blog writer "apolgizes [sic] for any error." Someone says her niece is a bright girl, and "whatever she does she will exceed." My former neighbor, a lovable Mrs. Malaprop, broadcast that she had had an auptopsy following her mammalgram.

To one obsessed with words, any inscription anywhere can cause dizziness by over-thinking. A sign attached to a light on a causeway admonishes us to "Watch for pelicans when flashing." Yes, a pelican could certainly do collateral damage to a person who is flashing. Another on the bottom of a sorghum mill says, "Feed cane large end foremost." A café sign in our area beckoned travelers on a cold day to "Come in and have a hot bowel of chili." A church name on a billboard says it all: "St. John's Holy Tabernacle Church of God in Christ."

An innocent speaker can make us blanch. A child says his name is Maalox. My aunt in a mobile home park reports that her trailer is parked on a cully sack. A seeker says he is going to look up a puzzling word in his catharsis.

By now, my literary friends are saying, "By golly, I didn't know ol' Jan was so bedeviled by the language." Actually, nothing could be farther from the truth. I am comforted in all this merriment and confusion by the observation of the Polish writer Czeslaw Milosz, whom I once had the pleasure of interviewing. He said, "What is not said tends to nonexistence." Being bombarded by all this naming and misnaming stuff, I know, by extension, that I am alive.

Jan Seale: A Writer at Work

Story Circle Network: You're a much-published author, Jan, and it's clear that you take your writing work seriously. When did you start to write? What, for you, is the relationship between writing and publishing your work?

Someone said that one didn't have to have an unhappy childhood in order to be a writer but it helps. I began writing as soon as I could read and write, probably because I had tuberculosis as a child. Just as all my friends were going to school and exploring the world, I was sitting in bed from ages five to seven entertaining myself. I still have a few of the books I read at that time, one in particular not a child's book but a sort of coffee table book with pictures of birds and poems about them. To this day, I can turn the pages of that book, glance at the bird, and recite the poem that accompanies it. As I memorized those poems, I remember thinking: I can write something like this. And I did.

I look on that time as a marvelous period in a child's life where words—reading, and saying, and writing them—actually saved her, kept her sane. And yet she didn't know any of this. She was only following an instinct toward something she would do and love her whole life.

Later, as a teen writing poems, I had a couple of friends who wrote poems too, so we had this pleasurable thing among us. My teachers responded appreciatively when I showed them a poem but there was no organized writing club in my school. In my love of words, I knew I was different from my classmates—but no one ever said, "Jan, I think you're going to be a writer."

I won a couple of campus writing contests in college. I was in seminars in creative writing at the University of Louisville and after I graduated with a B.A. in English, I began publishing poems. But surprisingly, I was also publishing articles on childcare. My first son was born seven months after I got my degree, and with him came articles on diapering, bedtime, telephoning the doctor. I found that absolutely ordinary ideas about mothering, common sense stuff, could be sold for good money. I teamed up with an OB-Gyn who wanted the byline but not the money and wrote a number of articles on patient/doctor relations.

After a few years, I went back to school for an M.A. Mine was the first creative writing thesis in poetry at North Texas State University. Then I taught a year at North Texas and began to see the possibilities of publishing poems and critical articles in academic journals.

....

SCN. In addition to working as a writer, you have taught autobiography and memoir writing. Tell us about this part of your life.

Teaching autobiographical writing came after I left the University of Texas-Pan American, where I had taught English for 12 years. When I quit, I thought I would probably focus on writing, but I found that I missed teaching. Also, I needed more income, so I developed a little "cottage industry" based on a perceived need in the place where I live.

Every year thousands of retired people winter in the Rio Grande Valley of Texas. With discretionary time, they seek out activities, and one such, just naturally, is telling the story of their lives for their families. So I developed a month-long, weekly series called "Writing Your Life Story." I taught it mainly at the Hidalgo County Historical Museum, which welcomed the traffic as well as the subject. I also taught classes in RV parks and retirement centers.

Now I've expanded my yearly Winter Texan offerings to two series of workshops, Part One and Part Two. Generally, people take Part One in January and Part Two in February. Sometimes I teach multiple classes.

I also teach one- and two-week workshops in autobiography at other sites, such as Ghost Ranch in New Mexico, West Texas A&M in the Summer Writing Program, and at Mo

Ranch near Kerrville. Often I give one-day workshops, and hour-long presentations to groups like genealogical or old-timers clubs.

I teach creative writing too, both locally and elsewhere. And lately I've been giving a workshop on women's wisdom called "Celebrating Women's Gifts." I've just come back from Maryland, where I presented this topic in a weekend workshop at a retreat center.

SCN. What are some of the satisfactions you gain from teaching memoir writing? Have you experienced many frustrations?

Adults, particularly older people, are ready to learn; they receive information eagerly. They may have the gifts of wisdom, compassion and patience, enabling them to hear their classmates' stories and respond helpfully. They also know how to take what they hear from others and apply it to their own stories. And they often hear themselves telling their own stories for the first time to others and may make a wonderful discovery in the process. I love to feel that I have helped bring people together to let this magic happen.

But there are frustrations. The hours together are far too brief, and time limitations in class inhibit people's freedom to tell and hear stories. How to share 70 or 80 years of one's life? Another frustration: Here in the Valley my students are not permanent residents, and when I teach away from home, I am the itinerant one. I may never know whether our time together helped them to complete their stories.

My teaching relieves the loneliness and constant self-starting of writing. I can rise from my desk, take my lesson plans, and move out to a definite time and place. The teaching also takes me to environments of interest and allows me to study human nature.

While my students' life stories contain fascinating facts and turns of event, and often inspire and amaze me, I've not been much tempted to appropriate them in my writing. They have their stories and I have mine. I don't claim any virtue about this, but when I reflect on it I think it's probably best that it's turned out this way. I don't mean to imply that there's a strict line between my teaching and writing. But the way the teaching influences the writing is more a general thing for me. My time with students shapes me as a person in subtle ways that will allow me to write with more feeling, from a broader experience, and with that kind of awe for the human condition that a writer needs.

SCN. You've written a handbook for memoir writers. How did that come about? You've also self-published it—could you share your thoughts on that process?

I laughingly say I wrote *The Nuts-and-Bolts Guide to Writing Your Life Story* when the handouts for my classes became too bulky. After years of teaching memoir writing, composition, and creative writing, I realized I'd acquired more than a few tricks in my bag. I wanted to write a book that students could use when they left the class, or as a substitute for taking the class. The other self-imposed requirements were that the examples would be drawn from older adult experiences and that this how-to book would actually be fun to read and use.

After it was published, I learned that students in freshman composition were using the technical chapters on spelling, grammar, and punctuation.

As for the self-publishing, that was not my first choice. (An agent shopped it for eighteen months and got two offers of contracts but we decided against both). The self-publishing has proved satisfactory in that I keep much more of the profit from the sales than I would if I'd gone through a commercial publisher, and I control the distribution. I always have them on hand and can do anything I want to with them. We're in the 6th printing now—I print 100 at a time with a local printer. The book goes with me to all my seminars and classes. Depending on the arrangements with the sponsors of the event, it can be a required text or a supplement.

Self-publishing has polished its halo lately, and I think it's one of the healthier trends in publishing today, especially as it's an answer to the mega-publishing houses which call books "products" and pay the writer poorly. (Distributors really irritate me, gobbling up another 15%, after the 40% wholesale discount, off the retail of a book.)

To publish one's own writing allows a writer to get on with disseminating her work, but she must have the means and energy to promote and distribute it. That's the trade-off: you get more of the profit, but you have to work harder after publication. I dislike this aspect of self-publishing, but I was willing to do it because I believed in the book and I needed it desperately to teach from.

SCN. Some of us are poets, others essayists, others write fiction. You seem comfortable in a variety of literary forms. Tell us about this, please.

Poetry: Whatever I write, I always return to poetry. It's the most satisfying way for me to write. I think of poetry as my mother tongue, my basic artistic language.

Short fiction: I began to write short fiction in earnest while I was teaching at Pan Am because I was teaching creative writing and the curriculum required students to write a short story. I thought I should be writing my own, along with them, to experience what I was putting them through.

And then a beautiful thing happened. I found out early on that certain stories in my heart and mind could be told much better in prose than in poetry. So the same thing happened when I was 35 as happened when I was five, alone in bed all day with a book of poems. I read and read and then put the book down and said, "I can write one of those."

I had beginner's luck with the second short story I wrote, called "Jack of Hearts." (It's in my collection, *Airlift*.) The story was chosen by the PEN/Syndicated Fiction Project and published in 1983 in seven major newspapers, including *The Chicago Tribune* and *The Kansas City Star*. In the decade following, seven stories were chosen for this project. These are traditional stories that appeal to the general population. Two of the stories were presented on National Public Radio.

I have a new manuscript of short stories that I've begun submitting. It may be hard to get them published as a collection because many of the university presses, which are the ones daring to print collections, want experimental stories for academic readers. I had to smile the other day when I received a kind rejection from a university press editor in which she declined my stories because they were "plot-driven."

By the way, I'm probably one of very few fiction writers who is not too eager to write a novel. I have written a formula romance novel (unpublished—written on a dare), and I have the beginning of another mainstream one that I might get around to finishing some day.

Essays: This is one genre which literally sneaked up on me! I have written columns for newspapers, one called *Living and Other Complications* for a local paper, another for the *Corpus Christi Caller*, and for a while I wrote a 4th of July piece for the *McAllen Monitor*. One day I looked at my clips from these and other sources and realized I had a book, which became *Homeland*.

As I get older, I seem to write more essays. For one thing, by now, I've been witness to hundreds of folks writing their memoirs, and have been privileged to read some gorgeous accounts of personal experience by my students.

Our memories and mental faculties change (notice I used "change"—not "decline") with age; we learn to draw on our vast experience and to feel confident in speaking the truth of our lives through essays. As I get older, I think my will to invent, to use ideation in really fantastical ways, has waned. I'm looking on this as an opportunity to explore other ways of thinking and writing.

Research in liquid and crystal memory interests me, particularly as it reflects the mature mind and memory.

I'm also interested in the newly-identified "creative non-fiction" (now about 10 years old). It's fascinating how much artistry can go into this kind of writing and a growing attention is being given to the form and shape of it.

Much of my published writing, maybe 80 percent, is shaped from my life experiences. Sometimes the fun of using them is in trying to be as honest as possible (in essays or poetry) and sometimes the pleasure is in seeking to alter it—disguise, re-do, add to, take from, mix and match—for a more satisfying experience for the reader (in fiction or poetry). Of course, everything anyone's told me, and everything and everyone I observe are also "my" life experience. When we consider the principle, that's a pretty big reservoir for all of us to draw on when we write out of "our personal experience."

I haven't the foggiest idea how I would write science fiction; I'm not much of a what-if thinker. And I refuse to help students in my writing classes with it because I'd be poorer-than-poor as a guide in what has become, the little I know about it, a well-developed stylistic mode.

Outside of poetry, I think non-fiction is the easiest to break into print with. I am constantly urging my students to send this or that account to this or that publication. When they take me up on it, they are often happily surprised at its acceptance. My students' writing has been accepted in large-circulation magazines and anthologies. This is rewarding to them, and me.

The biggest problem for students is deciding that they can take rejection if it comes. I try to model that hurdle, telling them about the poem that was rejected 21 times before it was accepted, and about the short story that came back with a big "Just a memoir" scrawled by a peptic-challenged editor across the first page, only to have it later accepted by *The Yale Review* as the fiction it was intended to be.

SCN: Your work was honored with an award from the National Endowment for the Arts. How did that feel?

My fellowship with the NEA was awarded in 1982, for poetry. I took that year off from teaching and just wrote. I finished a book of poems (*Sharing the House*, riverSedge press) and started several other things. The fellowship was a huge affirmation of my writing and I am forever grateful to have had it. That year made me realize that I was not going to get as much writing done if I continued to teach fulltime, so I'd better begin to think how to get more writing time. Yes, it was a watershed experience.

Part Two: Creations and Re-creations

When old words die out on the tongue,
new melodies break forth from the heart.
~Rabindranath Tagore

Published in *The Mesquite Review,* Sept/Oct 1998

Confessions of a Genre Jumper

A review of a biography of Rose Macaulay, a British author born in 1881, suggested Macaulay's work had not survived because she had throttled herself on variety: historical novels, comic novels, travel books, with a voluminous correspondence to boot.

I hope Rose Macaulay's reviewer was wrong, that other factors, like the quality of her work, bad timing, or a fire in her library denied her a decent literary following. For I too am a genre jumper.

From childhood well into adulthood, I was solely a poet. After a couple of books of poetry, I began to notice that I was breeding narratives that wouldn't yield themselves to the economy of poetry. Stories went for walks in the margins of my poems.

What could it hurt, a little flirtation with fiction? I had heady beginner's luck. The fourth story I wrote (two in school, one for a little magazine) was accepted in the prestigious national PEN Syndicated Fiction Project, which ran through the 80s, accepting each year some 40 stories out of several thousand submitted, to be featured in the Sunday sections of big-city newspapers. My story, about a small boy on Valentine's Day, was chosen by seven large dailies with a combined readership of six million. I made $1200 on the story. I was hooked.

In the introduction to *The Poet's Story,* a collection of prose by prominent poets, Howard Moss, the late poetry editor of the *New Yorker,* observes that a poet writes facing a mirror and a fictionist writes facing a window. If either would write in the other genre, they have to understand that they are "seeing through a glass darkly" and overcome this basic difference through something called "style."

Maybe Rita Dove, Erica Jong, Raymond Carver and a host of other writing luminaries can switch disciplines without penalty, but many American genre jumpers continue to be fined for straying out of bounds. The poet who writes a story with an

43

episodic or non-conventional plot is dubbed suffering from lyricism, "scattered." The lines of a short story writer who tries poetry are labelled "plodding." And in a sub-category of this literary Puritanism, the playwright who is not an actor is viewed as an inexperienced outsider.

Are genre jumpers an anomaly of the present age? Of course not. Shakespeare the poet writing plays? Coleridge the poet writing essays? It's curious that some critics are bothered by literary cross-dressing today.

One reviewer of my short stories, maybe to give credit but not too much, noted that I had "dabbled" in drama. A dilettante of the stage? Funny, it didn't feel like dabbling when I was at work on the two full-length plays that have seen production. Still, when I met with resident dramaturges for critiques and rewrites, their sentences were peppered with, "Of course you're not an actor so you wouldn't know . . ." and "It's just like a poet to . . ."

The bottom line is that there are poem ideas and there are story ideas, some with dramatic implications. I usually feel a story as a story, a poem as a poem. (A dramatic idea has to knock me down with its genre rightness—otherwise, too much work, too much time and risk to venture writing a play).

If I can't get hold of an idea, sooner or later I ask myself if I'm in the right genre. Or, as an eleven-year-old who once lived in our household (and had never studied media-message theory) said at the supper table one night as the boys were discussing a school project, "You know what way to fix an idea by what the idea is."

Sometimes a story is so hard to tell that I find myself laboring just to put down what the story is not. Moving the idea to a poetic form may be the answer. The metaphors and symbols are jostling to be first in line when the gate opens on the poem. If I'm skillful enough, I bring the fictionist's art of transitions, suspense, and denouement.

Maybe a poem is asking for more and more specifics. It wants to stop and describe the carpet; notes the glistening saliva in the corner of a character's mouth; sees a rat diving under the refrigerator, an old calendar on the wall from . . . what year?

That idea is a goner for a poem. It refuses to knuckle down to specific rhythms, intensified vocabulary, interesting syntax, the certain truth that a poem demands. It's metamorphosing to a story, hopefully taking along the one-two punch of poetic intensity.

Occasionally I'll do a sideways move within a genre. Once when a children's book contract went awry, I took the story and turned it into an adult memoir which then became my fifth story in the PEN Syndicated Fiction Project.

Right now on my desk I have a story which came from a poem, which is in process of going back to a poem. Kind of like marrying the same spouse a second time. Another poem, a long one about a dog, an animal which poetry editors don't seem to feel as intensely about as I do, is on its way to the story farm.

Sure, there are stories and poems, but what about a novel? Genre jumpers may, just may be able to redeem themselves if they manage a novel.

Years ago an acquaintance said to me,"When are you going to write a book?"

Thinking of my latest one, *Airlift,* a published collection of short stories, I stammered,"Well . . . I have a' ready."

"No," she said,"I mean a real book, a novel." She charged on."Then *Reader's Digest* might condense you."

"It's an idea," I said meekly, picturing myself as a tiny can of condensed milk.

I like Grace Paley's answer when she was asked in an interview if she considered herself a citizen who writes or a writer who is a citizen. Paley replied,"Oh, I don't know . . . I just think of myself as a person."

What I'm interested in lately is the blend of short fiction and essay. Several of my stories presently remain in a Sargasso Sea of invention and memoir. They are what I say they are, fiction or non-fiction, on a given day when I'm sending work out.

But, someone asks, hasn't it always been so? We dip out of our lives for making our art. What about the lawyer novels and the romans à clef and the initiation stories? Still, what I'm moving toward, wanting to write, is a kind of small short-story-looking "piece" where tension increases by means of a two-step between the testimony of real life and the comeliness of art. I want the reader to be piqued that the story doesn't take comfortable lines, that is, rising action, with complications from a basic conflict—and then to be profoundly disturbed or satisfied, or both, by the conclusion. The closest examples I have encountered are from the writings of Sherwood Anderson, particularly his wonderful short story, "Death in the Woods."

....

Genre-jumping pales before the steeplechase of content. Hurdling over fact toward whimsy, I worry that I am becoming a pathological liar. Will my heirs trust my autobiography after they've read snippets of same in works labeled fiction? Conversely, am I moving, here in later life, toward the essay because my ideational faculties are dimming? That's how I read it on bad-hair days. On good days, I call it wisdom.

Whatever. From the top of the fence, where I'm sitting, the view is not bad, not bad at all. I'm privileged to keep my ambivalence as a genre-jumper.

Published in *riverSedge,* 1989 and *Appearances,* 2012

Comparison of poem "Afternoon on the Larkspur Ferry" and short fiction "After Long Silence"

Some time back a story of mine was published called "After Long Silence" in which three cousins meet for the first time and spend the day together in San Francisco. They are very different—two are from the Bay Area—one urbane, sophisticated, traditional; the other urbane, sophisticated, lesbian. And the third is a visitor to the area—a woman from the Southwest.

It started out as a poem but the size got unwieldy because I wanted to give more details. Besides, long narrative poems are harder to market to literary journals than short ones. And the very specific details I wanted to work with did not lend themselves to the language of poetry. The story idea lent itself to prose. In prose, I was not so much tempted to overdo the passion nor to dally with poetic rhythms.

So I rewrote the narrative poem into a short story and was much more satisfied with it because I was able to develop a tone and a style that I couldn't achieve in the poem. I'm not saying that someone else couldn't; I'm just saying that it wasn't in my realm to say what I wanted to say by means of a poem.

Notice in the story ending how much more finessing and detail are possible in the prose version. Also, note that I changed the point of view from first to third person. The wide-angled lens seems to fit the setting better.

First, the poem:

Afternoon on the Larkspur Ferry

Here we are, keeping a date of thirty years,
two California cousins and their Texas one,
women sprung from three Arkansas brothers.

We meet at the landing, eye each other
before we embrace, our solitary selves
rushing out to our sisters by blood.
We stride three abreast like giant paperdolls
unfolded from the complicated origami
of our last three decades
and mount the stairs of the ship,
then dart fore and aft, excited as children,
warming to the connection.

Now the windjammers sail by. We name them
as we have begun to name our children
left at home, or those leaving us at home.
We bless them, scattered and free over the earth,
or safe in a grandmother's harbor for the afternoon.

San Quentin, my cousins point, a place of sealed lips—
we see the dark glints in each other's eyes,
some maximum securities we are locked in,
some life sentences yet to be commuted.
Alcatraz. Sorrow trapped, the perpetual waves
of an inland tide, old useless islands
 we can forgive but not forget.

We dock, and disembarking in midsentence,
triple off through the park. In the hotel elevator,
we learn each others' fears.
One must stand away from the glass;

one can only stand near it.
Now turning and turning in the revolving restaurant,
we go into family orbit—our children and mothers
and fathers and husbands sparkling and winking,
passing in and out of sight, growing dull,
cutting, caressing us.

We drink our sweet punchy drinks
passing them in a circle for samples.
And thus our lives, a sip of regret here,
a gulp of advice there, a slow, savored observation,
a sudden bubble of a joke.
None is willing to drink too deep,
to drown herself and the others
in an afternoon too private.
We exchange the origins of children's names,
symptoms and remedies for the family disease,
lost childhoods and loves, vacations,
professions, schedules, but not a single recipe.

High above Market Street, we begin descent,
meet our boat, the sweet sadness
creeping the downside of our afternoon.

Back aboard, we sit on the open deck,
revive ourselves in the spray,
looking from one to the other,
daring who will chicken out first—
ruined hair? sore throat? soaked clothes?
No one gives in, uniformly stubborn,
upholding that trait of the family.
We laugh, compare our politics,
find we are unanimous and give low hoots.

At the cars, we stand a long time
in the late golden afternoon

unable to break the magic
as though hovering at a fire
that keeps us alive.
There are hugs all around.
There are rehugs
and then we go, cousins,
back to our places on the wide earth,
carrying the secret of our genes,
the delightful knowledge
that past our kinship—the similar bones,
the slant of eyes, the shape of noses
we are friends.

Now the short story:

After Long Silence

Have they dreamed their meeting as hand-holding dolls unfolded in an origami family? Call it the prison of kinship. After thirty years, excuses played out, they meet: three women sprung from three Arkansas brothers.

Annie and Jill live in the Bay Area. They have done a few funerals and christenings; otherwise, they stay kin by phone. Today they meet Marie, the visiting Texan, the one who never moved West, young woman.

The Larkspur Ferry landing park. The Californians politely wreathe their Texas cousin. Marie forgets, does a double abrazo. Her sprayed hair rebounds from Annie's environmental cheek. Her cream foundation momentarily catches a wisp of Jill's flying brown hair. They stand back for another eyeing. Marie's yellow cotton greets Annie's beige wool, Jill's menswear.

The Californians bring the Texan to heel between them. They stride three abreast, knowing they have only the afternoon.

Up the stairs of the ferry. Dart fore and aft on pretense of finding three seats. Call, beckon one another. Anything to conceal this family voyeurism.

The whistle blows and they set sail across the bay for San Francisco. Marie puts her hood up. "You're cold?" Annie asks. She turns to Jill. "Marie's actually cold."

Annie thinks they should warm their Southwest kin with California wine, comes back sloshing three rosy glasses. A sudden lurch splashes Marie's white tennis shoe. Annie is sorry, so sorry. Marie dismisses it, toasts her wine roughly, like keg draught: "Bonding rites."

Windjammers, and it becomes important to read their names. Soon there's migration to the names of children, spouses, exes: Mandy, Paul, Keith, Suzanna . . . on and on, so many they bob away, toys on the waves.

The Californians point: San Quentin. A block, a huge jutted stone, a place of sealed lips. They recognize the glints in each other's eyes, maximum securities, life sentences yet to be commuted.

Now Alcatraz. Old useless sorrow trapped. Perpetual waves of an inland tide wearing it away, but not in their lifetime. They are silent, thinking of things back home they plan to forgive but not forget.

The ferry terminal. Disembarking in midsentence, the cousins triple off into the little downtown park. People smiling, soaking in the precious sun, nodding and tapping to the jazz trio. Marie lags, lost in the flute. Her cousins indulge her, lighting on the edge of a planter whose flowers they discuss as possibilities for their walkways.

In the elevator at the Hyatt, further indulgences. One must stand away from the glass; one can only stand near it; the third endures all the fuss in bemused silence.

The revolving restaurant sends them into family orbit—mothers and fathers, especially fathers, and other cousins passing in and out of sight like the landmarks of the changing skyline.

"Wait!" the Texas cousin says. "What if there's an earthquake? What do we do?"

"What if?" says Annie. Her ex is an earthquake-stress specialist.

"Scarlett here," says Jill. "I don't think about it."

They order, just for fun, a Honolulu Lulu, a California Lemonade, a Texas Tea. They make rules: When the restaurant completes a quarter turn, retain your straw, slide your drink to the cousin on the right.

"Wow!" the California cousins say, in turn, when they encounter the seven liquors of the Texas Tea. Marie squinches her eyes, shudders at the sweetness of the West Coast drinks.

And their lives . . . a sip of regret here, a gulp of advice there, none willing to drown them all in an afternoon of private sorrow.

They exchange symptoms and remedies of family diseases. Jill received the nerve malady; Marie got the bad guts. They speculate on the chronic depressions of their grandfather, his "blue spells," their grandmother called them. Annie says the area of clinical depression in the left frontal lobe shows up blue on the computer. They toast the prescience of their teetotaling grandmother.

Annie sniffs. "Are you wearing Manly?" she asks Jill. "And if so, why?"

"It's not exactly sex-change surgery. My therapist says it's okay."

"Therapist?" It slips past Marie's lips.

"I've had the same one for eight years now," Jill volunteers. "I nearly croak when she goes on vacation."

Marie can't help it. "Eight years? Lord! Whatever for?"

Annie answers this time. "Self-esteem. Achieving personhood."

Jill shores up the line of defense. "Yeah, Marie, and how are you coping with midlife?"

Marie looks down toward Market Street. "Everything must curve up," she says in a dream. "And shine. Lips, hair, breasts." She pauses and looks at them. "Psyche too." They slide their drinks to the right.

Next, it's lost-in-childhoods. The time Jill was literally lost, in Tokyo, at six. The Collie pup lost for a while on the train between Annie's and Marie's. Lost together from their fathers in the Herpetarium in Dallas. These are easy losses to say. But the others: lovers, husbands, children.... Then a sudden recovery to vacations, professions, schedules. But not a single recipe.

High above Market Street, a sweet sadness prowls the downside of the afternoon. The three women gather their things and descend. The boat calls through mist now, and they retrace their steps in alley shortcuts. Two hours ago, strangers passed this way.

Aboard, Annie and Jill wonder if the late afternoon fog will be too much for the Texas cousin. "Nah," Marie says, eager to demonstrate heartiness.

So they find three seats on the open deck, the spray strong and cold when the boat gets underway. They look from one to the

53

other, daring who will chicken out first. Ruined hair? Soaked clothes? Sore throat? No one gives in: stubbornness shines through the genes. Fog blocking out the landscape, they gently turn to politics, compare recent votes, find they are unanimous, give low hoots.

At the landing park, they linger, leaning on their cars to steady their land legs. The fog has moved on, the afternoon turned ancient gold.

Rituals of leave-taking. This time, not the polite yoking of neck and shoulders. This time, the gravity of map and calendar making one body heavy against the other. Enfoldment: long legs matched, belt buckles touching, firm settled breasts in apposition—a reminder that one day they will be each other's only mothers.

A standing back, a promise to write, a quick deft secondary round of embraces. And then they go, back to their places on the earth. Past the chains of family, of ills and sins and maiden names, they have bested themselves.

They are, of all things, friends.

Five Versions of a Poem

circa 1990

I. The Lie of it

The night is August.
A little air stirs the curtain.
Startled by strollers, down the street
a dog bawls out. The fan is nodding
its idiotic approval on medium high.
A child, alienated by the heat
at the end of the couch whines,
In a way I wish it was a cold
snuggling night.

For all we know
the clock has stopped,
the earth halted in spin,
inertia hung. Tomorrow the fan
will be just as agreeable,
the sun blast and drill all day,
thirst be our only emotion.

Tires will squeal,
dog feces steam,
and locust churn
in the noon trees.

It's knowing the lie of it:
This heat will last forever,
keeps up willing ourselves
alive.

II. The Lie of It

A night in August.
Air, only air, stirs the curtain.
Startled by strollers,
a dog bawls out. The fan is nodding
approval on medium high.
A child whines
from one end of the couch,
wishing it was a snuggling night.

For all we know
the earth is halted in spin,
inertia struck. Tomorrow the fan
will be just as agreeable,
the sun blast and drill all day,
thirst be our only emotion.

We have no future but
squealing tires,
steaming dog piles,
locusts churning in the
noon-only trees.

Someone's lying to us.
Start the clock please
before we all agree
to hold our breaths
and die.

III. (a fragment out of dissatisfaction with I. and II.)

The heat is the dream—
something I'm angry about.
It makes my throat sore,
boils me in air,
is in secret friendship
with mosquitoes.

I awake.
It's important to feel guilty:
I consider the trains to Belsen,
blame my marriage,
the children,
my parents,
the country—
and lie there
in a black huff
unable to beg forgiveness
when a wind springs up,
unable to decide if
the heat's a metaphor,
or the weather.

IV. The Lie of It

August heat, a bad dream
full of bawling dogs,
fans nodding on medium high.
We awake boiling in air,
on trains to Belsen.
Guilt is important.

We've taken stock
in squealing tires,
dog piles,
locusts churning
in noon trees.
We've blamed our marriage,
children, parents,
the country.

A child whines
about snuggling.
The earth has halted
in mid-spring,
struck by a case
of inertia.
Someone's lying to us.
Someone's halted the clock.

We begin to make suicide pacts,
agree to hold our breaths.
We've forfeited lovemaking
for the duration.
Finally we can't decide
if heat's the weather
or a metaphor.

V. Sneaking Suspicion Grows

August heat.
A bad dream
crawling with locusts,
fans nodding yes
on medium high.
We awake boiling in air—
last call for
trains to Belsen.
Guilt is important.

We forfeit lovemaking,
buy stock
in squealing tires,
dog piles.
We blame our marriage,
our parents,
the country.

Now we're sure
the earth has quit,
struck down by inertia.
Someone's dandling
the clock.
A child is arrested
for snuggling.

We begin
suicide pacts,
hold our breaths.
But wait—
we're too confused
to act. First
we need to know:
is heat

the weather
or a sign
of things
to come?

Commentary on "McCully's Sod House"

This is a poem I wrote years ago after visiting a sod house still standing and on display in Oklahoma. I was fascinated by the brochure picture of the family that built it and were living in it in 1897. I wanted to write a poem but couldn't think why I should write a descriptive poem when all I was doing was just going over in words what I saw in the picture. We should be careful about writing poems that do no more than describe a scene or object as a normal human being might see it, especially in a photo. But I launched into it anyway, and just at the end of the poem it became clear to me what this poem meant—that is, what the deep truth of it was that I needed to know. And that truth was that it was the spirit of this man and woman, their gritty determination in the face of terrible hardship and danger, that charmed the house and preserved it to this day.

McCully's Sod House
(Aline, Oklahoma)

You are walking toward her leading a horse.
She is faced front, the child beside her in a dress
also facing front. She has managed a white apron
but is holding a chicken. She is bent at the waist.

It is 1897. You have gathered everything you own
for the picture. There are six cows and six horses—
some could be rat-tailed mules. Even now on the right
a helper steps from behind his team
to be photographed by the itinerant photographer.

The house is in the center background.
It is a half-acre of stacked-up buffalo sod grass
ripped from a mile away and hauled in by wagon.
For the roof you have split black-jack logs
and laid over more sod.
                              She has sewn flour sacks
together for a ceiling cover. This retards
the raining down of snakes, dirt, and insects.
A sod plow and a buggy complete the scene.

The life expectancy of a sod house is 12 years.
No one knows why yours lasted 60.
Some say it was the presence
of a large elm on the south.

Maybe it is the way you have chosen
to put your left foot out for the picture.
Maybe it is because she went back
to the soddie to change her apron.

short story published in *RE:AL, XXIII*, 1998
and in *Appearances*, 2012

Commentary on "Take Cover, For Instance"

"Take Cover, For Instance" is not about avoiding flak in wartime, though it probably would have been accepted for publication more quickly had it been. When I started it, I thought it was about a bedspread, a too-fine white candlewick spread given to my mother by rich people, on which I as a child spilled indelible India ink. This unfortunate event occurred on the same day there was, in our house, a miscarriage by a guest. So I thought the piece was about blood and ink. (Right, you're saying, those poets go heavy on the metaphors.)

As I wrote, I wept for the way my kind mother had not flogged me senseless for that particularly vile indiscretion against her one item of luxury. As writing so often does, in the telling was absolution.

Then I realized Mother was preoccupied with the miscarriage and she not only didn't punish me, but she neglected to tell me what was going on. I stood in the hallway most of the day with my finger in my mouth, totally befuddled by the womanly goings-on. So then my righteous daughter-self rose up to deal with the difficult pasts of mothers and daughters. And I thought the story was about common forgiveness.

I went on with it, page after page, telling what happened, or I thought happened to the spread: how Mother never used it again; how she gave it to me when I needed extra cover for my little ones; how it made a throw for an apartment sofa when one of those little ones went off to university; how maybe that was the bedspread sacrificed beneath the car at the beach in an effort to escape a high tide; or no, the one we covered a badly injured man with after a road accident; or how—if you choose to go with me further into the willing suspension of disbelief, there were several other scenarios for that bedspread. It took on a life of its own, as I smoothed out the reality, kneading the facts and yeasting them with fictitious elements.

I thought I was through with "Take Cover, For Instance," had rounded it out, zeroed in on the theme of nurturing, traditional women. I was preparing to use it in a reading at a university when, on the preceding Saturday, I volunteered to help my son with a yard sale. (Enter, nurturing traditional woman.) As he laid out old linens, I saw the amorphous bedspread—or a part of it—he'd cut out one side to re-cover some throw pillows. Just to be sure I was not dreaming, I spread out the remnant on the grass. Forty-seven years later, three black ink stains. Three old sins.

I took the bedspread-that-would-not-die on the airplane, and then up high in a library building to a room filled with rare books where the reading was to be. At the end of "Take Cover, For Instance" I drew it from its sack. There was a long collective sigh from the group. The word made flesh, the flesh literally cloth-ed. Afterward I heard a student in conversation with his teacher ask, "What was that, an essay or a short story?"

"It was an essay," the professor said emphatically.

But the story was later published as fiction. You never know.

Now I'm thinking of incorporating the yard sale into the story, which will change the ending altogether. For maybe the story is about progeny, about passing along mistakes, about the sins of the mothers visited upon the children. Or is it about pied beauty? Or mutability? Or immutability? Is it about everything I've ever thought it was about, and more? Can I let the multiple forms of this story—essay and fiction and memoir, as well as literal tattered bedspread—teach me?

Take Cover, For Instance

Once, sitting in bed, I slit a new blanket as I tried to cut a piece of construction paper, fighting the torque of my mother's sewing scissors with my awkward left hand. Of course, the blanket's looks were ruined and my mother was angry. But the story I am telling now is of a different bed covering, a bedspread. Sometimes the web of memory catches it as Snow White's picnic cloth. The chipper bluebirds take its corners in their animated beaks and hold it up as backdrop for a movie title. Other days, it is that hallowed cloth in the lore of religions let down from heaven or raised up to it, full of prayer objects or holy animals. My grandmother would say it had character. True. The bedspread was unique, not inferior, to flesh-and-blood creations walking through other stories.

*****

My mother's bed smelled of talcum powder. It was my father's bed too, but he was a lump on the other side, snoring quietly when I came in the pre-dawn, trying not to startle my mother as I touched her. "I had a bad dream," I would whine. Mother never asked me what it was about, only "Well," and opened the covers to receive me. I knew to crawl in and turn away in the curve of her arm. "Make a spoon," she'd whisper. I fell asleep again immediately and slept safe until dawn. Today, I acknowledge she was an adult, had done a mountain of work the day before, had an agenda the next day. Today, such a child as I would be counseled, scheduled for a sleep clinic, dosed with a drug at bedtime. Mother took me in, night after night.

Came the day a young woman of our acquaintance was put to bed in my parents' bed. Her illness, I was told, was ladies' troubles. Actually, she was about to miscarry.

I think Faitha must have been a young missionary, probably up from Central America on furlough. We were a way station for such. They would come for a week, the husband preaching on

Sunday morning, the wife demure in the second pew. She would be allowed to speak that night, her talk introduced as a devotional, not a sermon. She would talk about the women and children, how children raised other children, how she combined Bible study and nutrition classes in their apartment living room, and, in the end, how God provided everything she and her husband needed for their stay on the mission field.

The words of the missionaries brought dread. They brought us the news that God was holding us personally responsible for saving the world from hell. These people were doing what we weren't.

There would be an invitation to go. "The fields are white unto harvest," the husband would shout when the choir paused between verses of "I'll Go Where You Want Me to Go, Dear Lord."

My father, as hosting minister, looked anxious and sad and expectant from his stance in front of the altar table. Once I asked my mother, if I surrendered to be a missionary, would Daddy be happy. She said that wasn't a good enough reason.

Anyway, I knew I couldn't surrender to be a missionary. What would I do if I had a bad dream in Africa?

It so happened I was home from school the day Faitha miscarried. I had had a stomach upset the night before. Mother believed a person should stay quiet for twenty-four hours afterward, so I had to content myself with playing bed games all day. But I begged until Mother let me go in and sit beside Faitha on the big bed, that is, if I promised not to snuggle in beside her but to remain on top of the bedspread.

Faitha was on my father's side of the bed, her legs supported by a pillow. She was a dainty thing, very pretty, I thought, with long reddish hair and wavy bangs. She seemed to be just lying or sitting there, not really sick; that made two of us who were perfectly all right with nothing to do. Faitha let me comb her hair.

The bedspread was a beautiful Belgian-made white cotton one with candlewick texture and a heavy hand-tied border fringe. Only now do I have the words to describe it. Then, it just was, but even a young child knew it was too nice for the parsonage, that my folks could never have dreamed of buying it. The banker's wife, the richest lady in town, had picked it out and given it to us, probably in gratitude for some ministration of my father. It had a kind of sanctity.

When Mother made the bed with it, as she did on holidays or when we had company, the whole room looked like a department-store display. The spread was so heavy and white it graced everything around it like prayer or snow. I liked to dig my fingertips into the thick raised double diamonds and figure eights of the design and extract them slowly, allowing for an instant of delicious entrapment by the tight nubs.

On this day, this one day that holds in my memory like those tenacious hobnails of my mother's best spread, I excused myself from Faitha's sweet company for a moment and went into my father's study to take from his desk drawer a bottle of black India ink.

Maybe I had borrowed it before. Maybe I thought it, with its curious curved dropper shaped like a tiger's claw, was something I could not do without for the picture I was drawing. I am sure of two things: I wanted to impress Faitha, and I did not understand the permanency of India ink. I brought the ink bottle back to Faitha's bed and spilled three blobs the size of quarters on Mother's beautiful symbol of gentility.

Faitha had her eyes closed and I quickly lapped the spread over so the ink didn't show. Then a curious thing happened. When I went off to play somewhere else, Faitha apparently turned on her side and, getting a little of the spread tucked between her legs, bled profusely on it.

Later that day, Faitha called sadly from the bathroom for Mother, a long time the two women in there, I standing in the dark hallway regressively sucking two fingers, listening to Faitha's crying, Mother's murmuring comfort. At last they came out, Faitha trembling and crying, white and almost collapsing as Mother helped her walk. Years later, when Mother told me Faitha had miscarried the fetus into the toilet, I burst into tears. But what I thought of then was the bedspread.

For now, Mother restored Faitha to her bed and I carefully watched Mother's face as she pulled her prize, blood-soaked, from the bed. When she saw the India ink, her mouth opened wide, then closed, and she cast an angry glance toward me, for she knew immediately what had happened. But she checked herself and didn't speak, deferring at the moment to Faitha's anguish.

She soaked the spread in a washtub, first in cold water, then in a bleach mixture. Faitha's blood came out; my India ink did not. Not then and not ever.

So Mother put the spread away, folded on a closet shelf for years, still heavy and luxuriant, still stained, still too good for the rummage sale. I know she was grieved. The spread was one of the few objects she had ever been able to take pride in without the guilt of vanity.

***

When I married and hadn't enough bedding in a cold climate, she gave it to me. "Here," she said, in the only reference she ever made to my transgression, "it's got your signature." She smiled, a guarded teasing smile at the edge of memory.

Later, summer evenings, my kids lay on the spread in the backyard. They delighted to imprint their faces with the designs, trooping in to bath time bearing its pocky signature on their cheeks. They further delighted in the three firm black spots of India ink, a reminder that their very own mother had once been a foolish, careless child.

The bedspread fought on and on. Now in a second generation, it refused to wear out enough for me to give it away. Next it attended state university with a son. I have a vague vision of it draped over an old couch in a college-town makeshift apartment.

But I get ahead of myself. Sometime in the life of the spread, I ripped the heavy, tied fringe from it and trimmed a poncho. It was a period in my life when things I loved were slipping away from me, and I was comforted by the constancy of the fringe on my long walks, drumming against my thighs in a steady rhythm, not letting the garment twist on me or billow out when the wind stiffened.

And then the poncho took on a life, or rather, wrapped itself around one. We were high in the mountains of Tamaulipas, observing a feast day in a village we had hiked to from the main

68

road. (No, I was not there as a missionary. Was I still too afraid of my dreams?)

The poncho lay so well on my shoulders that I knew immediately when someone behind me fingered the edge. I turned and saw an old woman, a *viejita*, with a tangle of children around her. Seeing her shiver—maybe in fear, certainly in cold, I found it easy to slip the poncho over my head and hand it to her. But that's only an edge of the story. The bedspread itself was, by this time, traveling toward a dual destiny.

Sometimes I remember it, after its college stint, in the back of our van on the way home from a picnic. We come upon a fresh accident. After my husband has pulled the man with the opened scalp from the window of his boiling overturned truck, we lay him on that spread and swaddle him in it against the onset of shock. When the ambulance comes, does the spread go to the hospital with him, or remain along the roadside? Nights, lying under a more modest coverlet, I can fill a blank in the dark, wondering which. Times like these I would go to my mother if I could, pretending the simple question was a nightmare.

Other times, I know without a doubt the bedspread was the covering that launched itself one night on the tide. We were camped on the seashore, thinking we were far enough up into the dunes. Our sleep was thick from a day of ocean air, and when the water stole in around our cot legs, we were a while waking. Only then did we discover a number of our camping items had moved out to sea, stolen by the moon.

In this memory, it is Faitha's and my bedspread, and Mother's—always hers of course—peaking with the waves, riding like a joyous surfer, sticking as close to the waves as the moonlight. It is out past the second sandbar, irretrievable, undulating like the bedding a simple good housewife might billow over and over when no one is around to watch. Just for the pleasure of seeing it float on air. Just to make the morning calm, after a night of tears and remorse, or sweat and love.

Regardless of its end, the memory wraps me in the white of mourning, grieving that the dreams of my mother could not be realized, remorseful that I canceled out such a simple one, pride in owning a fine thing.

And do the words of the story pronounce their own truth, say that, sometimes, ink is stronger than blood? Say how inked words on a page may carry the soul of a long-ago unborn child once more into the light, place it tenderly on a candlewick spread, gather a mother, her young daughter, a friend around it? How a story can be at once resurrection and absolution?

Story first published in *Coe Review*, 1996

On Long Titles

One of my short-short pieces of fiction, published in *Coe Review*, has for its title a thirteen-word clause. When my right brain first proposed that heading, my left brain denounced it as outrageous for a story of 250 words. But I ended up keeping it, for several reasons.

But first, the story:

How the Neighbors We Never Meet Move and Leave Us Lonesome and Sad

Across the alley, the house is still up for rent, though it's been a year since the people moved. We intended to go over, ring the bell, offer a plate of brownies. We never did.

Once, a woman ahead of me at the postal window gave the address. She was blonde, anorectic-looking. She wore a desperate orange tan and four diamond studs in each ear.

Midnights, there were arguments poolside. Soprano sobs that begged to move back to Mexico City. Guttural answers delivered in thick English: They could not, would not.

Discussed also were his unfaithfulness, her nervous condition, their miraculous son. How they shouldn't get this drunk. And things, always things, that would never work out.

This lasted through a summer. In the fall, a moving van came.

But the man and the woman left remembrances. A white-hot security light that comes on at dusk and illuminates our bedroom like the eye of God. A poolside phone braying like a jackass night after night.

When it begins to ring, we awaken and lie holding hands, listening to its cry and trying to make sense of the patterns of white light on our walls.

I say, "Some night I'd like to climb that fence and answer that phone."

You say, "Maybe it would be them, just checking on things."

So I practice."Hello?" I say. "No one's home." I pause. "Oh, hi there—it's you!"

* * *

So why did I give the story such a long title? When I finished it, I noticed that it was as much about the "we" as it was the "they." (We should let the stories we write teach us something.) The paradox in the title shows a basic lonely sad place within us all, whether drunkenly quarreling poolside or lying in bed making little jokes. The messy length of the title echoes the inefficient way we labor to get things right. The title functions as a riddle, and also as an answer—that there is no answer in our lonely search for perfect communication.

History of "Santos and the Tree Warriors" and "A Private Miracle"

I wrote this story in 1976 after experiencing a hurricane and seeing a small boy walking down a sandy road pulling a bottle on a string and talking to it as if it were a pet. As I worked on the plot, I realized that the story was about fear of the unknown, coping, and intergenerational love in family life.

I submitted "Santos and the Tree Warriors" to a publisher of children's work in 1976, which rejected it.

It was first published in *The Valley*, a riverSedge Press anthology of stories, poems, and art in 1979.

I rewrote it as a fictional adult memoir, renamed it "A Private Miracle" and it won an award in the PEN Syndicated Fiction Awards in 1988, one of 45 chosen over the nation. It was published by *The Village Advocate* in Chapel Hill, NC on Sept. 25, 1988.

In 1992, it appeared in my short story collection *Airlift,* published by TCU Press.

The Mesquite Review published it in 1997.

Finally, it appeared in an anthology *Texas Weather* published by Lamar University Literary Press in 2016.

Santos and the Tree Warriors (Children's story)

Santos walked down the orchard road to the mailbox. On a string behind him came Perro, a big green bottle. Perro made lines in the sand. Having Perro made Santos feel braver.

Santos stopped to watch the red ants drag a crumb toward their hole. A few of them ran over his feet. He stood still and felt brave.

A lizard ran by. "*Ligartija!*" he shouted as he chased it. Lizards were nothing to be afraid of.

But as he neared some tall trees, he shook all over. The older folk called them palm trees. They called their leaves "fronds."

Santos thought they were giant warriors. And their leaves were headdresses for battle. There were fourteen of them and they were as tall as the buildings in San Antonio. They marched in a long row beside the road to the mailbox.

Santos led Perro into the grass and patted him. "Wait right here! I have to hurry the rest of the way!"

He turned up his collar and put his hands over his ears. Then he ran as hard as he could past the huge gray feet.

Santos took the mail from the box, put the letters between his teeth, spread the newspaper over his head, and ran back. He stopped to get Perro and look at the trees. "Yipes!" he said softly. "Perro! Look at the warriors!"

Most of the time, the tree warriors faced the ocean, their headdresses moving behind them in the breeze.

But if a storm was coming, they turned around and danced into the north wind while their fronds rattled. "They're doing their war dance!" Santos said.

He smoothed the letters, re-folded the newspaper, fixed his collar, and started for home.

His grandmother was sitting on the porch. He ran toward her. "Here's the mail, *Abuelita!*"

She took the letters and looked quickly through them. "*Gracias!*" she said, then began to fan with the newspaper. "Santos, the air feels hot. I think a storm comes."

Very late that night, the family listened to the radio. Then Papá rose from his chair. "So! A hurricane! Get my hammer, *hijo*!"

Santos ran for the hammer.

Papá took boards and nailed them across the windows.

Mamá banged in the kitchen. She said, "We must fill every pitcher and pan with water in case the pump goes off."

Abuelita looked in drawers. "I'll get the candles. Maybe the wind will blow out the lights."

Finally Papá said, "Now we are ready. Let's get some sleep."

But Santos was too excited. He called, "Abuelita!"

His grandmother came to the door. "What is it, Santos?"

"What will the hurricane be like?"

So Abuelita came in and told Santos stories of all the hurricanes she had lived through. She told of one where the wind blew so hard that the palm trees leaned over and swept holes in the ground with their fronds. At last she said, "Look at me, m'ijo. I am very old. No hurricane ever hurt me."

Santos was glad she had not been hurt. He was glad she could tell good stories. Soon, all the things he was glad about turned into sleep.

In the morning, the wind blew hard. The sky glowed green and gray and it rained sideways.

Santos could not go outside. Mamá would only let him stand on the porch and peek between the boards.

He spied the tree warriors. They were doing a super wild war dance. The fronds on their headdresses whipped and slapped in the terrible wind. They dipped now this way, now that.

Santos shivered all over. He was glad he did not have to go for the mail!

The wind blew all day. It rattled the windows and sent pieces of the chicken house flying across the yard. It tore down the banana trees and stripped the leaves from the ash tree. A bale of hay walked across the yard like a yellow straw monster.

In the night the wind stopped. The next morning Papá pried the boards off the windows. Mamá looked out and said, "I see all my chickens."

But then it began to rain harder. Abuelita said, "In every hurricane I was in, it rained and rained afterward."

Papá said, "Santos, I can't drive the truck down the road. It's too muddy. You will have to go for the mail."

Santos did not want to go. He would have to hurry in the rain. It would not be like days when Perro could go part way with him. He could not stand in the ant bed to make himself brave. But he put on his boots and raincoat. Mamá gave him a plastic bag to put the letters in.

He started down the road alone. The rain was like thousands of little stinging pins. The ant bed had washed away. This was no time to look up at the warriors.

Suddenly Santos stumbled. He slipped. He started to fall. Something big and rough took up all his space. When he finally quit sliding and flopping about, he was lying on a thing as round and hard and huge as a giant's leg.

He slung the mud from his hands and got to his feet. He stared down. A long gray pole stretched to the mailbox.

Santos leaped back. "It's one of the warriors," he whispered. "The wind blew down a warrior." He began to tremble. Then he turned and started to run for home.

But he stopped. "I can't go home without the mail! Papá will ask me why."

He spun around and headed toward the mailbox. His boots went Sluck! Sluck! as if they were trying to hold him back, but finally he was there. The top of the tree lay over the mailbox. He would have to push through the warrior's headdress to get the mail! Could he do it? He shut his eyes and made his hands into fists and took three deep breaths.

"Aiiieee!" he said over and over as he climbed through the fronds. Santos paused in the middle of the fronds and looked closely. "Oh, you are old and wet and sad," he said to the tree warrior.

Then he carefully put his arms around the fallen tree's neck. He thought at first he was measuring the tree but it turned out to be a hug. His hands did not even touch. He felt very small but he was not afraid.

He looked back at the other warriors. Their fronds were drooping, not standing out proudly in the wind as they usually did. The trees looked down.

The next day when Santos went for the mail, the sky had brightened. The orange trees in the orchard dripped rain. Five ants crawled around looking for their home.

76

Right off he saw the tire tracks where workers had taken away the fallen warrior. He stopped. He shaded his eyes with one hand, holding on to Perro's string with the other. The warriors looked toward the ocean. Their headdresses fluttered behind their faces. Everything seemed to be right with them.

"Hello, all you!" shouted Santos.

And then he turned to Perro. "How would you like to come all the way to the mailbox with me today?"

Perro did not move.

Santos spoke quietly. "There's nothing to be afraid of." And so Perro went, making great squiggly lines in the wet sand.

A Private Miracle (Adult Story)

When I think of miracles, I think of the one that happened to me when I was a boy of five. As other children, I had my own fierce secret demons—beings I did battle with when I was alone on the dusty road between my house and the mailbox, or in the dark of my bed on the screened porch of our house in the middle of an orchard, or in the midst of my friends at the Head Start program where I went to learn English. Maybe I had more than my share because I did not have any brothers or sisters to divide the unknowable and secret world with.

I was not afraid of the usual things—my parents, the dark itself, death—though I had an inkling of death because there was no grandfather to match my grandmother, my dear *abuelita* who lived with my mother and father and me. No, my worst demons lined the boundaries, the fields and roads around our home deep in the Rio Grande Valley of Texas.

When the wind blew in from the Gulf, as it did most of the time, the regiments of giant palms looked out to sea, their headdresses lazing behind them. Times like that I dared to look up at them through slatted fingers. Yet their heads were so high I could see their tops only in silhouette against the suncrazed tropical sky.

But when the wind came from the north, they took on the awesome personages of full-blown warriors, savages glaring down at me, pitching their wildest war dances and looking as menacing as the face on my Big Chief tablet.

It was on one of these gusty October days that I was sent to the mailbox a half-mile down the road, the last part of the way lined with the terrifying beings. I could not bear these mandatory excursions without my pet, a big green bottle I pulled behind me on a string. Perro had a knack for distracting me with squiggly lines in the sand as he followed me. Besides, he made me infinitely braver.

That day I did my usual ritual. Before I came to the palms, I stood in the red ant bed, sidling in so I wouldn't disturb them, then watching them explore new paths over my feet and legs. It is one of my earliest memories of machismo.

I led Perro to the side, coiled his string carefully, and said, "Be a good Perro! Wait right here!"

Then I turned up my collar, clamped my hands over my ears, and ran like the dickens past the huge gray feet of the warriors. Safely to the box, I put the letters between my teeth, spread the newspaper over my head, and headed back for Perro.

But a curious object stopped me on my way. I remember the shock of discovery as if it were yesterday. It seemed a large greenish-yellow fan had come to be lying in the road. I picked it up and turned it over and over, wondering why I had missed it going the other way. Perhaps I knew, deep down, that it had shaken loose from the trees above, but, charged as all the world was to me then, it was a gift and a mystery. My childish bent for innovation took hold and I remember saying softly, "I know what. I'll take this home to Abuelita."

So I tucked the fan under one arm, smoothed the teeth marks on the letters, refolded the newspaper carefully, found Perro, and thought of a song to whistle as I approached the house. My grandmother was sitting on the porch.

"Abuelita!" I called, running toward her. "Look what I brought you!"

"Ah . . . gracias!" she replied, with only a grandmother's intuition for what I thought its obvious use was. She took it and made wide sweeping motions before her face. "The afternoon is hot. A storm is coming."

That night, my mother and father left the TV on quite late to hear the weather bulletins. Papa hammered boards across the windows and Mama filled every pitcher and pan we owned with water. My grandmother laid out candles and matches.

Hurricane! It was a word of incantatory power and a torment I shared with the grownups. I was afraid to go to sleep that night. *"Mamagrande!"* I called, in the face of fear using the big name for her.

She appeared in the doorway, her gray hair framed in the light. "What, mi hijo?"

"Tell me about the hurricanes." To ask if this one would hurt me would not be brave.

She came to my bed and sat down. She took my hand and told me of all the hurricanes she had been through. At last she said,

"I am very old. You can see that no hurricane has ever hurt me." It was as solemn a pledge to me as if she had been God.

I was glad I had found her the fan. I was glad she could tell good stories. I was glad she was old, for the trust I could place in her words. Soon, and despite my pledge to keep a vigil, all the things I was glad of turned into sleep.

In the morning, the wind was blowing, blowing hard. The sky was green and gray and the sun seemed to have forgotten to come up. My mother would not let me go outside. She only let me stand on the porch and look out—and even then I had to peek between two boards to get a view of the savages.

They were doing a frightening dance. They pitched their bonnets across their faces, the feathers endlessly tormented by the terrible breeze, and bent farther over than I had ever imagined they could.

The wind blew all that day. It rattled the windows and sent pieces of the chicken house roof flying across the yard. It tore down the banana trees and picked all the leaves from the elm. A bale of hay went walking across the yard, end over end, like a yellow straw monster.

I slept with my grandmother that night. Sometimes now, dozing in a half-life, I can hear her say, "Hijito, it was hot with the windows closed. Did you see me fanning with my fan today?"

By morning the wind had stopped. Papa pried the boards off the windows. Mama looked out and observed that the hens had somehow survived. But then it began to rain. "In every hurricane I was ever in, it rained and rained and rained," Abuelita said.

My father cleared his throat. "I don't think I can get the truck down the road. It's too muddy. Mi hijito, you'll be going for the mail."

I had a thousand excuses, none of which made it to my lips. I put on my boots and raincoat and Mama gave me a plastic bag for the letters.

I set out alone, without the company of Perro, who would only slow me down today. The ant bed was gone, washed away. Coquena, my pet guinea hen, sat in an old orange tree fluffing herself. The rain felt like thousands of needles. I kept my head down.

And that was a mistake. Suddenly I slipped. I started falling all over the road.

Everywhere I tried to stand seemed unreasonable.

Finally I quit flopping about. I was sprawled on something as round and hard and huge as a giant's leg. Slinging mud off my hands, I struggled to my feet and stared down at what had stopped me. It stretched almost to the mailbox. It was one of the warriors. I turned for home.

But a few steps back and I heard my father's voice in my head. "Why didn't you get the mail?"

So I turned once again and, taking the far side of the road, hurried on. The warrior stretched one, two . . . five orange tree rows long. And at the end lay its head, crashed against the mailbox.

There is a longing in us to touch our fears, to make them ours by knowing them in all their sting. I reached out and touched the war bonnet, that thing which up until this moment had been a dark terror above me in my childhood sky. And that is when I knew the heavy feathers of my phantom warriors were simply palm fronds—green, brown, yellow—exactly like the one I had given my grandmother.

If even the innocent sin, I must have felt somehow my sin against the trees. I had the urge to make peace. And so I stooped and put my arms around the fallen palm's neck. Of course my hands did not touch. And then I climbed up on it and, stretching full length, lay there a moment, a moment in time that is a frieze in my head—a boy resting the sweet fears of his small existence on a tree fallen to earth.

From here on, the story is but a blessing and an amen to the miracle. The next day when I went for the mail again, the sky had brightened. The trees in the orchard dripped rain from their waxy leaves and ants crawled around, reviewing the damage to their mound. The highway people had come early that morning and taken away the fallen warrior.

I remember, when I came to the palms, stopping, and, halting Perro behind me, looking straight up at the trees. They were gazing benignly out toward the ocean again, their motion lazy and gentle.

"Hello, all you!" I shouted. And then I turned to Perro to see if he'd like to accompany me the whole distance.

He hesitated, that I remember.

"There's nothing to be afraid of," I said.

So he came with me, making new lines in the fresh wet sand.

Journal entry preceding poem "After Sunday"

San Miguel, 1992

In the pre-dawn, I heard voices coming across the plaza—low laughter and light feet—I peered out our window across the way, and saw 10-12 boys looking as though they were waiters, in black pants and white shirts. They were coming from work. They crossed the plaza diagonally and came out from under the laurel trees, appearing in groups of 2's and 3's. One gave a loud coarse catcall and the others laughed. They descended the steps and crossed the street diagonally and were gone. It all took no more than minute but they made me euphoric. I thought of the young waiter in "A Clean Well-lighted Place"—how he urged the old man to go home because the waiter had a wife to go to and wanted to close up.

I went back to bed smiling. An epiphany. Some part of me travelled with their feet, descending the city, light on the cobblestones at the secret time of day.

Why does so much inattention to little things amount to charm in their totality?

Published in *Isosceles*, 1997
Also in *The Wonder Is*, 2nd edition, 2012

After Sunday

      on the plaza
starlings shimmer the laurels,
sustain the love of novios
      parting to separate beds
at midnight.
Later, the cold before dawn
brings low laughter and feet
running light on the stones.

They emerge beneath the knitted trees,
young waiters newly freed from drunks
in well-lighted places. Now a catcall
confirmed by clapping, low words.
In twos and threes they jump the steps
to the street, their white shirts
luminous as angels by lamp's light.
They pass under open windows,
are gone.
      Only a moment, mágico,
a dream handed the roused sleeper
to lie quietly in, try to recall.

Were they here, these boys,
their small night joy published
on the starlings' wings at dawn
as the whole world's joy?

Commentary on Poem "Big Bird Comes to the Valley in 1976"

Shadowy totem figures, religious icons, weeping plants, and preying monsters are ever with us down here in the Rio Grande Valley of Texas, and they arguably make life more interesting than in more mainstream locations.

In the case of "Big Bird," I first presented a paper at the 1978 Texas Folklore Society meeting detailing what happened in 1976 when a giant bird was seen for several weeks at various places over the Valley. A folklore scholar told me at the time that an innocent observation I'd made in the paper was actually a well-known principle of folkloric activity.

It seems that when something extraordinary is explained away, it suddenly ceases to be reported by the folk. People quit looking; they aren't in tune anymore; their imaginations are out of work. The enchanted world steals off and in its place is the old rational, predictable one again. Myths feed on intense scrutiny of phenomena. Things happen because they are supposed to happen. Put another way, we may need to believe first, and only after that can we see.

The media used the mounting excitement of the myth for "the news" until they eventually killed it by "the news"—an evening TV report that Big Bird was only a mild solitary blue heron, strayed from its habitat on a little holiday from nesting. Newspaper headlines the next day definitively proclaimed the legend dead. "Big Bird" celebrates the excitement, variety, and pleasure of mythmaking. It laments the interference of commercial media which destroys this spiritual activity.

Like many of my poems, "Big Bird" came about quite a while after the fact. I wrote it twenty years later. It's not uncommon for many years to go by before I remember, in a different sort of way, something that happened and want to write it as a poem. Maybe it's that, after years of drifting, the deeper meaning lands in my heart.

85

The poem is a narrative, but also a catalog, and once the lists begin, they have to continue, since if they didn't, the rhythm and intensity would fall off disappointingly. The lines are quite long, to reflect the pile-up of information, to underscore just how high the myth soared, before the evening news deflated it. When I perform this poem, I must consciously take in big breaths to get through the lines effectively.

The stanza breaks were decided by the subject matter. The collection of details and the long lines require brief intermissions for the listener/reader. Purposely, the last stanza is longer than the others. I wanted the words to get slower, slower, and finally sit down on the porch steps with a small sad thump.

A poem should be more than a narrative, more than a summary or gathering of details, else why not tell the story in prose? There needs to be enlightenment and an inevitable conclusion, commentary without didacticism. The poem must gather intensity, presenting new and more alluring insights and sensations right to the very last. At the end, the listener should know, in both mind and senses, why he or she has given attention to the poem.

My Valley poems often incorporate Spanish, even at the risk of obscurity. The *cuentos de las lechuza* refer to stories of supernatural owls, notably totem figures of curanderas that have circulated for centuries in these parts. "*Viejitos*" is said with reverence for the wisdom that age infers in this culture.

Poem-making and mythmaking both involve an acceptance that there is more to life than meets the eye, that a secret world functions around us, guiding, giving beauty, excitement, feeling, and significance to our lives. Writing "Big Bird" was a great pleasure to me because the form and the subject naturally mirrored each other. It was one of those "clicks" that make a poet feel blessed in the practice of the art.

Big Bird Comes to the Valley in 1976

The color was white, silver, gray, brown, dark brown, black.
The height was four, five, six feet; the wingspan, twenty.
Otherwise, the bird was hairy, feathered, bald. In the pictures
drawn at school, there was the face of a bat, pig, monkey, man—
with pointed ears, eagle's beak, stork's bill, silvery red eyes.
"Pteranodon" and "pterasaurus" were librarians' nightmare.

The creature left footprints, hovered over a lagoon, hissed,
ransacked a tavern, terrified policemen, pursued children,
disappeared into a canal, perched on the Chevrolet company,
attacked two men (making one of them hot where it touched),
gave an unearthly noise, snapped its beak, ran into the brush.

There were T-shirts in four sizes and a song on a record—
the flip side an interview, old Japanese monster movies,
offered rewards and counter-rewards, vigilante groups formed,
words from the law on trigger-happiness, on endangered species,
talks about self-defense, bounty hunting, international animals.

At the end, the bird let itself be filmed in an orchard
with fifty people surrounding. Then the legend flew away.
The 6 p.m. news showed a mild blue heron gazing about.
The next day, its published demise: "Legend of Bird is Dead."
Soon the TV station had tossed the film, for more space—
(reports of drug hauls, bodies found in the Rio,
deaths of the prominent, arrests of molesters, murderers).

Then a haze clouded the eyes so the people no longer saw
the jabiru, crane, wood stork, brown pelican, condor,
and especially the great blue heron; even though these birds,
one or all, were here, in our midst: even though they came
to restore rumor, debate, declamation, the art of gossip,
the plucking of guitars, chills, *cuentos de las lechuzas*,
upstanding hair on the nape, children curved with respect
into the laps of the *viejitos* on front porches at evening.

Published in *Goodbye, Mexico,* Texas Review Press, 2014

Commentary on "Transfiguration"

During the "friendly" years of easy passage between Mexico and the U.S., my husband Carl, the musical director of the Valley Symphony Orchestra, was appointed by Gov. Dolph Briscoe to the Good Neighbor Commission. He had many delightful experiences taking the Valley Symphony on tour and also guest-conducting Mexican symphonies. Everywhere he went, Mexican audiences showed their excitement and appreciation for the music.

One such visit of his was a two-week-long conductorship of the Guanajuato State Symphony. During that time, after several days of rehearsing, the orchestra went on tour, playing in several Mexican cities, one of which was Salamanca.

Salamanca is located in the lower center of Mexico, population about 275,000. The petrochemical industry there has the largest Pemex refinery in Mexico. Because of that, its population is quite various, with engineers and business people coming from all parts of Mexico and beyond, as well as a class of service people, and, as in everywhere in Mexico, very poor people also.

My poem is the story of the concert at Salamanca. When I recall that occasion, my heart beats a little faster as I think on the magic of that night.

* * *

Contributor's Statement *Goodbye, Mexico*

I have lived in South Texas on the border for all of my adult life and have written much about the bi-cultural and natural environment. It is a very special place, with an exoticism of peoples, plants, and animals not found anywhere else in the U.S. Although our lives have been drastically diminished due to narco-violence, I cling to the hope that someday there will again be easy passage among our peoples.

Transfiguration
Convento y Iglesia de San Agustín, Salamanca, Mexico

I.
Entering under the plain streetside façade and looking up,
the fumes of the city's petroleum refineries lessening,
eyes adjusting to the dimness, one sees a new city,
this one of cherubim and seraphim. Apostles extend their hands,
bishops wield their mitres, Jesus and his mother ever suffer
amidst candles, crowns, leaves, and vines. The countless drapes,
sweet eyes, quiet wings, smooth feet are covered in pure gold.

II.
The Guanajuato Symphony sits ready behind the altar rail.
It is on state tour, with guest maestro, *el director huesped*
from El Valle de Tejas. Tonight they are playing Salamanca,
a post-Conquest city a-fume with oil refineries, industrialists,
cantinas, food vendors, and always the poor—booked into this
rare gathering place, a church begun in 1641 by Augustinians
and their indio converts, finally dedicated in 1706.

III.
Seven p.m. and by the guest conductor's compulsion to his gringo watch,
it is time to begin, the polished instruments hungry for their notes,
thousands of practice hours itching in the fingers and lips of the players.
For an audience, there are five scarved *viejitas*, come lately off the street,
old women possibly here only for warmth, for rest, for succor.
Signal given, the concertmaster appears from the transept, back straight,
refusing dismay at the empty seats, this latest affront to his art.

IV.
Equally stoic, the orchestra tunes and the maestro crosses from the sacristy,
his formal tails blacker than the robe of the priest who introduces him
and his musicians, says a prayer of consecration to the glittering walls.
The maestro taps his music stand with his baton, raises his arms,
and as the poster on the streetside plaster wall has announced,
"Oberatura de la Opera 'El Barbero de Sevilla'" fills the empty nave.

V.

Following the final chord there may come with luck that blessed second
of silence wherein a listener transitions back into the world. Tonight,
in that interval and in this place, the conductor dreads for his players,
for Rossini, for himself the hollow claps of five pairs of old hands.
But when he turns to face this meagerness, here's a tsunami of joy,
sanctuary roaring approval, bravos, feet stamping the cold Byzantine tiles.

VI.

The sound rises, keeps on rising into the golden filigree of the ceiling,
for while Rossini reigns, the church has filled with folk silent as mice at midnight,
bowing to the niches, crossing themselves, sliding into the pews,
filling row on row in their own good time, come, after all,
to hear their symphony orchestra, to banish with strings and trumpets
and flutes and tympani the great hungers of their hearts.
They are bartenders, demimondes, nursing babes,
mujeres elegantes, doctors, street vendors, barefoot children,
teens coming lately in uniform from school, architects, nuns.

VII.

The director huesped wonders if they should start the concert over,
considering who has heard what, but now he presses on
with the program: Schubert's Unfinished Symphony, an oboe fantasia,
the finale as Ippolitov's "Escenas Caucasianas," each time
the people on their feet, with long clamorous applause and shouting.
This night is filled with the joy of the wide world—music of Italy, Austria,
Los Estados Unidos, Russia, played by Mexicans for their countryfolk
both *pobres* and world-renowned oil advisors of Salamanca, here
in the cocoon of Mexican Churrigueresque architecture
built by the Spanish Augustinians and their mestizos, here
in this nest of universe speaking in concert *en verdad*
the language of music through centuries and cultures,
all the while, golden saints and angels listening from above.

Part Three: Practice Makes More Practice

An essayist is a lucky person who has found a way to discourse without being interrupted.

~ Charles Poore

Babysitting the Imagination

This week you have been babysitting. Last week was a different week: you were an active professional writer. You did things in the grown-up world. You finished a story, sold another one, had a poem accepted for publication. But this week you are stuck. You are not going anywhere. You're sitting beside the playpen of your mind watching your ideas fuss, cry, giggle, roll about, doze.

You're staring at the computer monitor, pushing "delete," pumping the backwards arrow, writing lists, contemplating the hummingbirds outside the door, eating pretzels, drinking something cold. Asking yourself when this baby of a story is going to grow up. Asking yourself why this poem refuses to eat, why that one smiles at you so beguilingly that you stop short of a final definitive edit. Wondering what in the world you're doing with all these ideational children anyway. Reminding yourself that when one agrees to be bedded by the muse, one's got to take turns caring for the offspring.

Okay, so if you have to sit here hour after hour in childcare, how far can you go with this metaphor without ludicrousness? Pretty far, actually, and what better thing do you have to do?

Allow the baby to be the idea, incident, preoccupation, nugget, thought, dream, note scribbled on a napkin. How can you justify this long afternoon of slow-down? How can you get through the afternoon, or week, or month of seeming inactivity, stasis, being stuck?

For starters, we have the responsibility to be kind to ourselves as writers when we are not working at top speed, full of glorious ideas. We gently turn away the critics and shut out other well-meaning voices, recognizing the contemplative life is counter to the American way of work and materialism. Workers can be fired for daydreaming, children are told not to get off task at school, and everywhere one goes there is a TV to entertain when we might be sitting and thinking. In other words, there's value in sitting quietly beside the playpen, studying the baby—perhaps taking notes, making lists, journaling.

A good babysitter pledges to keep the child safe. The writer respects his/her ideas, believes that—at least for now—they are valuable and worthy of attention. They will not be trashed but kept in a folder for the future. The writer-babysitter promises the parent, in this case the left brain or "self" or alter ego, to care for the seed of the idea.

If the child is awake, if there is a possibility of liveliness, one may enter into play, allowing for some uninhibited youthful behavior. We agree that every detail doesn't have to be nailed down before one begins the story; that we may find interest in plot other than the one started with; that a different ending awaits; a new character jumps into the middle of things. If you give yourself over to the child, the time passes quicker.

It's good to remind one's self in the lean times that an idea will grow at its own rate. The incubation time may be different from our usual pace. The idea has a mind of its own. We trust that somehow, regardless of the tinyness, insignificance, helplessness and haplessness, this idea might flourish.

The writer's charge asks you to accept, as is, the unbidden preoccupation of its presence. Then it frequently surprises, with turns of thought, possibilities, details, memories, combinations of ideas. Take care of an idea and it will take care of you by entertaining you.

The thought may produce contradictory emotions. You may feel at the same time that it is both valuable and worthless. A baby cries but its neck smells sweet. A small child is naughty but charming, his brother's acting out exasperating but defenseless. At times you may be sick and tired of your idea. That's when you might consider valuing it beyond transitory feelings.

A small child is its own reward, is complete now, is not all potential. The ideational infant is an event rather than a task. So it doesn't become a novel; so you never get it published. You get practice by watching, tending, nourishing. You are better off for having practiced the art. You have paid attention, and that is your main job as you babysit the imagination.

Compiled from presentations made at Ft. Concho Literary Festival 1993, Rice University Writers Conference 1994, and Austin Writers League Workshop 2000

Shaping Real Life Stories Into Art

The British writer E.M. Forster in his *Aspects Of The Novel* points out that the observation, "The king died and then the queen died," is merely a sequence of events—a "chopped-off length of the tapeworm of time." On the other hand, add two words at the end of the statement, "The king died and then the queen died of grief," and you have a story. We are now interested in human behavior, values, and consequences.

How do we get from "just the facts, ma'am" to the art we are longing to create? Here at the end of the 20th century, we are seeing a great bleed-over of one genre into another, and especially a commingling of fiction and non-fiction. The present cross-dressing of genres doesn't promise to help readers keep their genres straight. The book page editor of a large metropolitan newspaper told me that many people call her asking if they might review a nonfiction novel, or worse still, to say that they are writing one. The term "autobiografiction" was recently used playfully in *The New York Times Book Review*.

Reporters win Pulitzer Prizes for interpreting facts; college creative writing programs offer courses in journal and memoir writing; television is rife with "movies" (traditionally considered fictitious) applying dramatic techniques like mustard plasters to the lives of real people caught up in horrific circumstances. Not long ago, a person said to me, "Don't you just love" . . . and she named a popular novel. I replied that some readers had reservations about it and gave her a couple of their reasons. "But," she countered brightly, "those reasons don't count because after all, it's a true story. Remember at the first how they told that it came about?"

Why, we sometimes wonder, do we even need fiction if we can reproduce fact so exactly? Examples of hyper-reality abound in video games, video and audio evidence presented in trials, photo finishes of horse races, instant replays of sports, and simulations of all kinds in virtual reality training.

There will always be a hunger for meaning beyond the facts. Picasso observed that artists tell lies to reach another form of truth.

When we strive to change what's in our lives—what we've experienced—into art, we are offering a new way of looking at life, both to ourselves and to our readers. We have a duty to make that new shape that we give our experience as deep and round and wide and intense as we possibly can, to give meaning to real life that all of technology with its virtual reality cannot.

Our question today then is, how does one deliberately change life into art? How do we go from an anecdote, a family tale, a confession, an adventure, a happening—to a short story, a novel, a play, a poem? The answer, of course, is "very carefully." Because if we say it is a fiction, and the bones of real life stick through, we're done for, at least in that piece of writing.

Maybe it's best to look at the similarities between those occurrences in our lives that someone (maybe ourselves) tells us would "make a good story or poem" and a story or poem we know as such, and admire. What are the common elements between an ordinary life-experience story and a work of the imagination?

Any kind of effective storytelling—poem or prose— has in itself engagement. It opens with a bang, a lead, an interest- getter, a hook, a grabber: "Ever hear the one about the . . ." ; "Something happened to me last night that I . . . "

In fiction, the opening asks much more of the listener than mere politeness. It may begin with description, or dialogue, or a philosophical discussion, or a generality, or a shocking disclosure. Sometimes writers writing directly out of experience try to get too much information across in the opening sentence, a little like asking a newborn to take a big bite of steak; the reader isn't ready. Here's an example: "It was 1934, Dad was dying, Jeannine had left home, Uncle Robbie was in town, and the azaleas had just begun to bloom." Let's admit it's a bit clever and even shows a kind of unstable hyperactive narrator, but it's a little too much to digest first thing.

A part of engagement is a recognition of and respect for the audience. The natural raconteur will ask for it rather openly: "Listen, my children, and you shall hear . . . " or, as one of my life-story writing students with a number in Huntsville for an address (the state prison) put it: "I am writing this so that all my family can understand why I acted as I did and will not do the same." The fictionist will ask more subtly, but still try for effective engagement in the opening first or second paragraphs.

Both informal and formal storytelling have flow. They move along. The campfire story goes from episode to episode; if the relater of the story is lucky, each of these true-life episodes will top the last one. In a piece of fiction, that rise is mandatory. In an artistic piece, like Cormac McCarthy's novel *All the Pretty Horses*, or the Frank McCourt memoir/novel *Angela's Ashes*, there may seem to be a charming randomness but the story is all the while moving toward a climax. Things have to get more and more complicated, bizarre, out-of-control. In good stories, there has to be conflict, and the conflict must get more and more conflicted until there is a solution, or the character has to decide there cannot be any solution. It stands to reason that if we're going from what really happened, to what might have happened, we have to think about rearrangement, about a crescendo of trouble, about the situation-conflict-complication-climax pattern.

An example of how this works is a fine story by Sara Burnaby titled "Bears" based on her preoccupation with bears in a time she lived in the wilderness. She writes, "In one year I had 7 encounters with bears, which even where I live, is unusual." And she enumerates these encounters: bears looking at her on the trail, walking beside her above on a ledge, in the meadow outside her cabin. In her story she begins with these encounters—seemingly all about equal in excitement, and tells them leisurely and like a philosophizing environmentalist. Then suddenly the story explodes with a plot in which the woman in the story tries to get even with a man that she hates—a bear killer—by moving to his housetop the very bait he has put out in an effort to lure a bear close enough to kill it.

Burnaby's story is a good example of a number of seemingly equal observations and incidents forming the prelude to a chilling plot. The result is art.

Stories, both naturally occurring and artfully made, contain in varying amounts tricks from the storyteller's bag, elements such as humor, surprise, irony, suspense, detail, emotion, staging that feed the listener's interest. These are at the heart of the skill of the raconteur. I never cease to be amused at Homer's line from the *Odyssey* where he says that Odysseus, on the night of his homecoming, had to spend the night on Penelope's porch incognito and that he slept "like a sausage turning over the fire on a spit." That line surprises me and is amusing and gives detail and spells out weariness and frustration. The powerful irony here? The great wanderer and warrior has been reduced to a wienie!

There's a dreaminess, a magic about both folk-told tales and created fiction. In this regard one of the most beautiful stories I know of is Sherwood Anderson's "Death In the Woods." The point of view in this 11-page story changes four times! I have never had the courage to be that bold but I admire him for getting away with it.

Listen to Anderson wrestling with the autobiographical nature of the story—or does he want us to think it is as artless, as feckless as he is leading us to believe?

"The old woman was nothing special. She was one of the nameless ones that hardly any one knows, but she got into my thoughts. I have just suddenly now, after all these years, remembered her and what happened. It is a story.

....

"It all comes back clearly now.

....

98

"(I wonder how I know all this. It must have stuck in my mind from small-town tales when I was a boy.)

....

"I remember now that she was a bound girl and did not know where her father and mother were. Maybe she did not have any father. You know what I mean."

Then there is a big middle section where the point of view goes to the woman, and then to an omniscient observer.

In this part the woman, the wife and mother of cruel men, freezes to death in the woods as she is on her way home from the butcher to feed her family. Wild dogs take the meat away. The boy in the story is witness to her frozen naked pristine body, his thrilling introduction to death and sex all at the same time.

Toward the end, Anderson completes the meaning. "The scene in the forest had become for me, without my knowing it, the foundation for the real story I am now trying to tell."

This story is a masterful example of combining a supposed personal history with artistic purpose. Magic happens.

Successful stories both natural and artificial finish well. The raconteur's story often has a stronger actual literal finish than the fiction writer's version, but the fiction makes up for that by disclosing some universal idea or theme. So as we the readers draw to a close of the artistic version, we are willing to settle for less literally because the bigger picture is opening up to us. The cosmic view mitigates the loss of the personal one.

Up to this point, we have been considering that personal history and literary event have many points of coalescence and that this idea of "life" over here and "art" over there is something fairly newfangled in the history of humankind. We continue to wonder if the animals depicted on the walls of Lascaux were for the aesthetic enjoyment of the dwellers, or to ensure their supper.

Or, as Kathryn Morton in a wonderful essay called "The Story-Telling Animal" puts it, "We did not arise from the ape with a sharp rock, or even from the one who learned how to sharpen a dull rock, but from the one who saw the connection between sharpness of rock and soon-ness of supper." Narrative shapes our lives. We are nothing without our stories.

On one level there is this inseparable unity of life and art, and writers are just the scribes. On another, writers in the new millennium who want to write stories that will wind up in print, preferably for money, need to make distinctions.

Material from our lives, which we use in imaginative writing, is not to be confused with confessional or inspirational writing. Confessional writing, the kind drawn from journal entries and support groups, usually doesn't hold up as fiction. If used at all, it needs to be greatly altered. Beginning writers, especially, shouldn't be misled by figures such as Sylvia Plath, Anne Sexton, Robert Lowell—the so-called confessional poets. Even now, after time has passed since their deaths, some of their material seems embarrassing and tiresome.

It's a new world, a world where social ills are reiterated, aired, published. Where no behavior is too kinky or evil or bizarre, or just plain dumb, not to be scheduled on a talk show. Where stories of sexual abuse, divorce, drugs or promiscuity, loss, and violence have been told and re-told.

When we take story material from our past, we want to do enough with it that it will transcend sensationalism. If we think we might be too close to our story—that is, so passionate that we can't control our work, we should delay writing, or try it from another point of view.

The heat of the moment is not always the best time to use one's life material. I sometimes spend 10 to 15 years thinking about a subject before I write about it. It takes me that long to make sense out of things that happen, to connect the personal with the universal. And also, I know if I can't get it off my mind, if I don't forget it, it's probably right for me to tell. It is not until the story owns me that I can claim it.

Material that's very personal is not to be confused with "cause" poetry—which was popular in the 60s and 70s. It's okay to write poems about whatever is troubling one in politics or the environment, but people who get into writing and use art only for their personal social opinions usually do not grow or stay with the creative process. They use art and then get worse, or quit altogether.

So, not "I am a poet because I oppose the _____," but "I am a poet. This poem is my take on _____."

I write poems on the environment, a cause with me, but I try to bring the same knowledge and skill to them that I would any other poem on another subject.

James Dickey withdrew from the American Academy of Poets because they admitted Russian poet Yevtushenko—whom Dickey thought was nothing but a politician.

Some of our greatest writers use social concerns as their subject matter (Paz, Mistral, Neruda, Milosz, Havel) but they are writers for life, not using art to serve propaganda.

Another important distinction for creative writers using life experience is to give careful thought to the form the new work will take. Will the material be a story, a novel, a poem, a children's story, a play? How does one make that determination?

Usually you don't have to decide among a big variety of forms just which one you'll adopt. Your material will tell you that it might be a story or a poem, or you'll be wondering if you have perhaps the complication and largesse of a novel.

As for story or poem, if the real incident is short on complication, that is, it doesn't have much of a plot and it has a metaphor that hits you in the face, and maybe some life truth that strikes you also, then you probably have a poem. Remember that in a poem, language rules, and rhythm is the crown prince. Form is second in line, and rhyme is third.

Conversely, if, in the original episode or event, you have a situation that has lots of ends and outs, lots of practical details or description, you may find you can say more with it as a story or an essay rather than a poem.

Poems can be about anything. Some notable examples: Ted Hughes' "To a Dead Pig," James Dickey's "May Day Sermon to the

Women of Gilmer County, Georgia Delivered by a Woman Preacher Leaving the Baptist Church," Mona Van Duyn's poem "Letters from a Father" filled with phlegm and constipation and high blood pressure, or Maxin Kumin's poem "The Excrement Poem."

And how does a writer make a choice between writing a short story and writing a novel? What you do is begin to write about your character. If you are finding that you do not want to let your character go after a 10-to-15 page short story, then you probably are looking at a novel, or a series of interrelated stories. As far as determining whether you have a memoir or a novel, you need to understand that generally a novel has an emphasis on the story, and a memoir emphasizes an identity. In other words, a novel needs a plot; a memoir can be just as long, and as charming, but it might be a series of episodes. Are there a number of important characters who require vast development, and does the action take place over a long period of time? Then the material needs the space of a novel.

When contemplating writing a children's story, you might ask yourself if you have some basic major elements. Do you have a character the child can identify with? Is there a conflict the child can understand? Is it fairly simply solved? And above all, is it satisfactorily solved for the innocent and trusting psyche of a child? More than for any other genre, I often have the sense when I hear an anecdote that it's a perfect story for children, almost as is.

For an essay, with the same material you're considering for a memoir or a novel, you might have some personal experience narrative, some observations about an aspect of life, some definitions, comparisons, contrasts, and most importantly, a theme or point.

And what about a play? If you keep envisioning scenes on a stage, you may have a play. Remember that in order to write a play, everything we say about the requirements of fiction—such as complication, conflict, resolution, characterization—all these have to be present in a play plus present in a framework of being acted out in a box over a two-hour time span; or in the case of a screenplay, in front of cameras, with time constraints of television programming or in competition with fantastic cinematic techniques being used today. You had better really want to write a play out of something from life to do so today.

In changing life to art, we need to look at two kinds of truth. One of them we need to avoid; the other we need to embrace.

The first kind, the one we need to avoid, is the kind where we tell everything as it really happened. In beginning creative writing classes, when students bring in their first short stories, there will almost always be a lot of irrelevant details in the action: a phone rings and it's the wrong number; dogs bark, a factory whistle blows, there's an auto accident or it rains or they see a friend from their hometown quite by accident in the train station in Rome. When I ask the authors what they intended by including these things in the story, they usually say, "That's what happened! That's the way it was!" as if the fact of actual reality was all the reason needed to justify their inclusion. In fact, these kinds of facts are dangerous. This enumeration of actual facts limits the reader's imagination and may cloud the meaning of the story or cause us to miss it completely.

The writing shows over-particularity. Too many details appear irrelevant; the writing is messy because "real life" is messy. In a story that has moved beyond real life, the particularities are selected out for their irony or symbolism, or their suggestion of universality, or how they "click" with other parts of the story. While seeming ever so casual, the details show intention. They signal, early on, that something has been done for the reader. Here's a gift; there's integrity behind it.

Nothing should be in a work of art except art. Art may mimic life but it's not a rubber stamp of it. Art has shape and intention and universality and layers of meaning. That's what makes it art! The facts that we choose to use in our works of fiction and in poetry must be absolutely 100% true as far as we can determine them for the situations we are writing about, but every one of them must be intentionally chosen, not randomly selected and inserted.

When the reader meets an image, an object, a happening in a story, there should be an underlying sense that its being there was pre-determined long ages ago. Someone said that if you're going to use an image, a symbol in a story, you should use it at least three times: the first time, the reader may or may not notice; the second time, the reader's subconscious says "Hmmmmm" and the third time, the reader consciously says, "Ah-hah!"

Sometimes our emotions hogtie us. When we try to be faithful to what actually occurred in the life experience, we may lose sight of ourselves as the writer, and when we've lost that, we've lost the art involved in making the story. When we're feeling disloyal to the situation we're writing about, we can remember that we are striving for another level of understanding in our re-telling.

The other kind of truth that we need to watch for, and embrace, is just the opposite from this first kind that we want to avoid. This kind is what I call "deep truth."

It's the meaning behind the meaning of what we write. Moving out from an episode, we are looking for motives, recognizing symbols, seeking the subtext. This is the truth that we're seeking to discover in the first place when we tackle writing the story. We turn something over and over in our minds and can't figure it out. So we launch into a story or poem about it, hoping that by worrying around with the ideas and words, we'll be able to make some sense of it. And we very often do. We discover things we didn't know we knew. We put two and two together and *Voila!* it is indeed four, sometimes five if the poem has an extra effect.

Be careful about writing poems that do no more than describe a scene or object as a normal human being might see it—even when it's in an out-of-the-way place. One pitfall of poets is just to describe, in which case, a photo would do about as well. There has to be interpretation, some way, usually not direct, but some way, for the poem to be worthy and effective.

We should remember that "personal experience" also includes the lives of those around us because simple observation of others, even if nothing happens to us, is an event in our lives. And if we practice "mindfulness," awareness of our observation of others, we increase our potential material exponentially.

Eudora Welty says she does not like to write stories about herself, only about those she knows, observes, thinks about. Her material comes from her close observation of people in the library or the doctor's office or beside the road. This close observation is certainly her "life experience" as well as anything else she does.

Some subjects lend themselves readily to fictionalizing: harrowing or learning incidents from childhood, eccentric characters, neighbors, life changes—initiation into adulthood, marriage, birthing, parenting, jobs, dreams, illness, loss of loved ones. Then, there are unusual surroundings, conflicts and problems, juxtapositions, and just quirky, weird things that grab us, observations we've never talked over with anyone else or read anything about.

For example, several women have told me stories of their shame at not being able to breastfeed their babies. In each instance, the feeling expressed was one of great sorrow, long-range mournfulness. I began thinking about writing a story that dealt not with the cliches of breasts as components of woman's beauty, or as sex objects, or as recipients of cancer, but breasts as objects of maternal pride, and their failing in maternity as a great common unspoken sorrow of women. Then I remembered a story my grandmother told me when I was a child of her failing at nursing her firstborn. Did I remember all those other stories and pay attention to them because my grandmother's story had lodged in my heart and mind? Or did I use Grandmother's story because it was a handy instrument on which to fasten my idea? It's hard to know. The point is that I had never run across a story with this particular theme. And so it was much more interesting to me to try to do something with. And it became the story "What Flesh is Heir To"—one of the stories in my first short story collection that people frequently comment on.

To share or not to share. We have borrowed from those around us for these stories. Do we let friends, neighbors, relatives in on our use of them? Do we discuss our depictions, ask them for details, for their permission to use, or for critiquing? It depends. The trickiest reader, or source for the research, is the person who has been there with us in the experience, or is the real-life prototype of the story.

As critics, relatives and friends are neck and neck for who is the riskiest. The writer Yi-Fu Tuan said, "Don't ever show an early-stage manuscript (if you can avoid it) to neighbors, relations, or clergy: their unconscious agenda too often is to dampen your enjoyment tools."

Friends? It depends on the stability of the personality and the relationship. Someone said—partly in earnest, partly jest—that a writer trashes all her friends by the end of life.

Several years ago I observed a nugget of a story in real life that fascinated me. I thought I'd like to try turning it into fiction. The story involved a friend of mine who has worsening Parkinson's and his decision to loan out his prized '69 Ford Mustang convertible to a young couple for their honeymoon. When he was well, he would never have loaned this car out. I wanted to involve the car only as a kind of prop for the larger theme of his changing values in the face of his disability.

I needed to know more about Don's car so I told him that I was writing a story with such a car in it and asked if he'd take me for a ride and tell me a little about it. This man is a retired full colonel whose last assignment was the Pentagon. His wife told me he did not read fiction. I thought I'd never get him stopped on the 320 engine and mag 500 wheels and the differences between the 1964 1/2 muscle car and the '69 version. He gave me detailing catalogs and charts of specs, and from time to time he'd drill me on the facts.

Finally, I had to tell him that the story wasn't exactly for *Motor Trends*, that it was about a man like him. He replied, "What is it anyway, a science-fiction story?" Then he began to ask, every time he saw me, "Do you have that story about me finished yet?" This put a lot of pressure on me, plus the fact that I wanted to write about what was going on in the head of a man afflicted with an incurable disease.

Weeks went by and self-permission to write the story grew fainter and fainter. Finally, I sat down and chanced it, thinking all the while about Faulkner's comment in *The Paris Review*: "If a writer has to rob his mother, he will not hesitate; the 'Ode on a Grecian Urn' is worth any number of old ladies." I finished it on July 4 and took it to him that night in a blue folder with a tiny flag on the front. And he liked it, *gracias a Dios*.

But I had paid an awful price for revealing too much of my plan to him, in this case weeks of indecision and uneasiness that I was going to alienate him.

The reward is that Don loves the story. He told me he couldn't understand how I knew exactly how he felt in his head about his Parkinson's. And that was the greatest compliment he could have paid me. Now, he and I have a deep bond, an understanding we never had before, and in that I'm just plain lucky with the chance I took. And that is the real reward for writing: the deepening of the soul.

Unless the depiction of a character modeled on a real person is favorable, it probably is best to consider changing a great deal surrounding the character—especially in this age of litigation. It may be that the real situation has put us in mind of an interesting theme. We can use that theme but make vastly different assignments to the elements of the story: changing the sex of characters, their ages, vocations, the numbers in their families, the setting; almost certainly shifting the sequence of scenes, changing the ending, or just adding an ending. The more you change people from real life, the more liberated you feel in writing about them.

We have to be prepared for people to see themselves in characters that we feel are wildly antithetical to them. In my play *Radical* two sisters quarrel and act cruel and immature when their mother is diagnosed with breast cancer. The real-life daughter of the woman I got some of the background material from for the fictional mother was distraught and angry when she read the play. She saw herself as one of the daughters when in fact, she was a foil, an exact opposite to the women in the play. Although I didn't feel guilty about the depictions and would not have changed them, I was sorry that Melanie had mistakenly identified herself with these daughters when in fact, she had been most loving and supportive of her mother.

And we have to be prepared for others to be flattered out of their minds by depictions that we're worried might be too frank. Generally be prepared to be surprised by our friends and neighbors' reactions, often including their total indifference to what we've written.

Finally, there's a tendency for us to be a bit skittish about the story, to de-value it, or lose faith in it, because we have drawn it from an incident in real life. We're feeling guilty anyway that we don't write more imaginatively, like say, Stephen King or Ray Bradbury.

I wrote a story several years ago based on the menacing presence of an old man in our neighborhood when I was a child. Almost everything in the story really happened but I rearranged the episodes for better flow and action, added things I thought would be effective, and put an interpretive ending on it. I enjoyed writing the story because I learned more about how being vaguely threatened all that time had left its mark on me, and I discovered in the writing a wonderful serendipitous thing: that the physical location of the incidents formed a square around the home of the girl, that all the places she was forbidden to go because of a possible assault by this old man virtually formed a wall around her, a prison wall.

What I discovered in the writing of this story was that I had harbored that feeling of being restricted in my movements as a girl, that is, hemmed in by my sex, not free—a feeling of danger that follows women all their lives. I wrote the story in first person, with a kind of past perfect sepia tint to it, the voice of a sassy eight-year-old but with an overlay of reflection.

It seemed to write so well that I felt nervous about the ease of it. I sent it off to the first place, a well-known journal for short fiction and soon got it back with the words "just a memoir" scrawled on the first page. I was badly unnerved by that, and my records show that I didn't send it out for almost a year. I considered trying to revise it but since I couldn't think of what to do with it, I left it alone and sent it out the second time. This time it was accepted—by *The Yale Review*. And it has since been republished twice.

In summary, we as writers are privileged people. We have consciousness as our raw material. We can agree with Sherwood Anderson in the story alluded to earlier,

"The whole thing . . . [the story of this woman] was to me as I grew older like music heard from far off. The notes had to be picked up slowly one at a time. Something had to be understood."

Maybe the bottom line when using life experiences for writing is whether we as writers can stay interested in the material. Do we want to learn, to make discoveries as we write? We may be shaped in real life while in the process of reshaping our lives in fiction.

Self-editing

A popular book published in 1992 sold almost a million copies and was on the *New York Times* best seller list for 99 weeks. There are 45 pages of acknowledgments and notes. And yet, in this beautiful book, which is revered by so many, the Ph.D. author misuses the verb "to lie" constantly, as in "The woman just lays there on the pavement." Most of us have certain expressions that we would dub "informal," such as "It's me," but in formal writing we observe the rules. So where was this author's editor?

Gone are the days when a writer speaks with complete trust of "my editor." Twenty or thirty years ago an editor working with a writer would fix spelling, suggest re-writes, re-order, and patch up grammar. Such help is rare now, with the writer expected to do most of this, granted, with computer help. The bottom line: a writer has to edit herself with every bit of savvy and wisdom she can muster before she ever sends out a piece. The polished manuscript will hopefully rise to the top of the slush pile. Every issue of popular writing magazines has an article about preparing a manuscript. Some deal with content, others with the mechanics.

First, a bit about content editing. The self-editing process really begins before you write because you exercise editing skills in choosing what you are going to write about. Write only on something you know about or are willing to spend time finding out about. If possible, make sure it is something that interests or excites you.

And be realistic about your experience when you consider your markets. Your subject may not win the day with the first five places you send it. Nix on the big markets if you haven't ever even tried the small ones.

As you no doubt have been told many times, don't worry about editing on your first draft. Just write. This works for most people. For others, they like to move slowly from idea to idea, re-reading what they have written and adding to that meaningfully and with full intention. That's okay too. After you have written for a while, you will learn which way works best for you.

Get it down, and as you go back over your writing, here are a few questions to consider as you check the content:

1) Are your statements accurate? Do you have the facts straight?
2) Are you happy with your generalizations? Are they true? Have you qualified them?
3) Are your language choices consistent with what you believe your audience will understand?
4) How about your logic? Do you move carefully from one point to another in your argument?
5) Have you kept your promises to your reader as outlined in your introduction?
6) Have you done what you started out to do, fulfilling your intentions?
7) Have you established a style—breezy, academic, colloquial—and kept with it throughout?
8) Are you conscious of the tone of your piece? Are you writing as kind, sarcastic, sorrowful, encouraging?
9) Have you observed a length consistent with the market you are trying for?
10) Have you considered realistically your readership's needs and tastes?

***

So, you've done your best on the content of your piece. What about the mechanics? Here's a checklist on those:

1) Right word: So many choices! The English language is rich in synonyms.
2) Spelling: Keep your Spell Check on. There are few excuses for misspelled words in this age.
3) Grammar: Loads of helps on the 'Net. Just ask Google a question.
4) Paragraph length: Five or six sentences are max.
5) Punctuation: Over-commaing is a frequent error. Watch out for apostrophes too.

6) Sentence completeness: Ordinary sentences take a subject and verb. If you write a fragment, be sure it's an intentional one.
7) Manuscript form: Get acquainted with the editor's checklist.
8) Repetitions: Read your piece aloud, trusting your ear to tell you when you've repeated a word in close proximity to its twin.
9) Consistency: Have you capitalized, abbreviated, italicized uniformly?
10) Credits: Give credit where credit is due.

***

Finally, in addition to the specifics above, here are ten commandments for successful editing habits:

1) Edit at a peak time of your bio-rhythm. Don't edit tired.
2) Copy-edit the final version in print form, return to the computer, print out, and read it one more time.
3) Read your copy aloud.
4) Read copy in sections, then read all in one sitting if possible.
5) Mark errors in colored pen.
6) When in doubt, enlist another reader.
7) Let the work ripen between edits.
8) Keep rough drafts and revision copies.
9) Avoid over-revising.
10) Know your strong points and limitations.

from *The Nuts-and-Bolt Guide to Writing Your Life Story,*
The Knowing Press, 1998

The Hang-up Nobody Talks About

As a teacher of autobiographical writing, I consider one of my jobs to be breaking down the barriers people set up along their paths to writing. One of these is the idea that recording their lives on paper constitutes the final act in their stay here on earth. When I mention this taboo in class, nervous laughter ensues. To some folks, writing one's life story is right up there with choosing a shroud.

Will our cells give up and shut down after we've completed our memoirs? Nothing could be further from the truth! If anything, personal storytelling enlivens and reinvigorates us. We're refreshed by recall.

No one of us is likely to get the privilege of designating the time, place, and circumstance of our leave-taking of this planet. Unless we are lucky enough to write, "And that is the complete story of my life," then lay down the pen and take our last breath, our life accounts will remain open-ended.

If, realistically, advanced age or a life-threatening illness puts a person on a limited timetable for recording their life history, I recommend they make lists of the most important times, people, places, and events of their lives. Thinking in small units, and writing single words or phrases on a pad rather than long sentences and paragraphs is within the range of almost everyone's abilities. These lists—without any other embellishments—will serve both as a legacy and a springboard for writing more complete memories as energy and attention permits.

Start a list of brand names you remember such as Ipana toothpaste, Jergens lotion, Burma Shave, and Fels Naptha soap. Under another heading might be listed "Firsts," such as first long pants, first high heels, first cake baked, or first fish caught. Where and when the "first" took place are often sufficient but significant.

Use headings to encourage your memory, even if you can't think of more than one or two items to begin with. Write at the top of separate pages in a small notebook such starters as "My Scariest Moments," "Memorable Birthdays," "All-time Favorite Books and Movies," and "My Heroines and Heroes." Leave plenty of space under each heading to add to your lists as new items occur to you. And they will! Trust your subconscious to be working on the categories. Even if you don't get around to writing about everything on your lists, the lists themselves are valuable keepsakes for your heirs.

If writing your life story fills you with the dread of finality, conceive of what you are writing as "Volume One." You may fill it with your memories up to the age of 18. My grandfather wrote a lively autobiography of 41 pages, stopping abruptly when he married. Family members teased that my grandmother kept him too busy after that. Even though it was brief, we have greatly enjoyed that growing-years account of his.

One student, Grant, chose a loose-leaf binder for his writing. He wanted to make sure there was room for at least 50 more pages because, he assured us, he had lots more living he wanted to do, then record.

Another trick to counter your anxiety and get on with the fascinating accounts of what has happened in your life so far, is to avoid the chronological approach, which has a beginning (your birth), a middle (your adult life), and well ... an end. Keep a notebook tabbed with subjects so that you are thinking of your life in terms of ideas, preoccupations, happenings, beliefs, and influences. Add to the subject areas as you think of new specifics and use the pages to help you get started on complete essays. This method can prevent stall-out.

Comfort yourself with the fact that memoir writing is not the exclusive province of the "mortality-challenged," as one student put it when we were discussing this problem of motivation. My autobiographical writing classes have ranged in age from 17 to 93. Third graders are being encouraged to write their "autobiographies" these days. Flannery O'Connor, the Southern writer, observed that if a person had lived to the age of twenty, there was already enough material to write full time for the rest of one's life.

Death claims one out of one of this world's population! Sobering, isn't it? But the statistic should not discourage us from celebrating the gift of life. We can remember and tell about the gift, knowing that our words will survive to bless ongoing generations.

Add Snap to Your Personal Experience Titles

A great title for your personal experience writing may simply occur to you. It's a gift from your muse. You'll recognize it as catchy, appropriate, even clever. Accept it with a big thanks.

Other times, when you've conscientiously worked through your writing and no title presents itself, you may be tempted to slap an easy generic title on your words. After all, it's your life, it's true, and it doesn't really matter. Resist temptation.

Be careful to avoid such prosaic headers as "Time," "Changes," or "Life." The other extreme is to be so explicit that you essentially give away all your candies in the title, for example, "He Finally Said He Didn't Love Me" or "My Little Girl Grew Up to Be a Neurosurgeon."

Some writers like to establish a title first. In fact, they can't proceed without one. The word or phrase functions to focus them. They can move ahead from there. But if a satisfying title does not occur to you up front, don't waste valuable time stuck on the problem. Move on and write your piece, then look back through it for a word or phrase that seems to epitomize what you tried to say, such as "holding on" or "joy beyond words" or "just lucky, that's all." Often these phrases or words literally jump out at you, like a stray dog in the woods. Grab 'em and tame 'em.

Can a title be too long or too short? It all depends. A specific single word such as "Weavings," "Sheila," or "Grunge" can provide the right touch for a chapter heading in your autobiography. Phrases that tease such as "The Moment My Life Stood Still" and "Horses and Headaches" can be effective. Short, pithy whole sentences like "Was I to Blame?" or "She Just Fished On" may be right for your purpose.

Perhaps you'll want to replace a section you first titled "Joys and Sorrows" (a cliché) with synonyms such as "Victories and Vicissitudes" or "The Pats and Pans" your life dished out.

Titles for chapters arranged chronologically often present the greatest challenges for overcoming boredom. "Early Childhood Memories" might give way to "Five Years Old Going on Twenty" for the youngster who grew up too fast (although one life story writer, whose last name was Early, had a great time punning on the first title!). "A-courting We Did Go!" is more fun than "Courtship and Marriage."

The title of your full-length autobiography should always be your personal preference but the less generic, the better. Titles like *The Story of My Life* or *My Memories* tend to pale beside more interesting possibilities. One writer, chronicling the period after he was married, called his book *After the Children Came,* emphasizing his parental role. Even with this title, he could flash back for several pages to his own childhood.

A *Patchwork Quilt of Saved Words* titled a book of various kinds of writing—letters, columns, speeches, and lists—which reflected the writer's life. *One War, One Crew, One Ship* is the account of the close-knit group of a writer's Air Force unit stationed in Italy in WWII.

For titles of book length, take a cue from a major theme in your book. A military wife, whose life story emphasized the many moves of her family, chose *Always on the Move* for her book. This title reverberated with various meanings, from moving around frequently, to the woman's restlessness and exceptional energy. She even used it as a touchstone for a final chapter in which she suggested old age would not catch her sedentary.

Good titles are like spices: they tantalize, hint at the essence of the entrée, pique the reader's interest and make him or her salivate in anticipation of what's coming. Dare to be a gourmet title-maker.

Remarks to Students on Poetry Day

There is a great cartoon that goes something like this: A person is rappelling up a steep mountainside. Another one, lower down and not outfitted for climbing, is stretching one arm up, holding several sheets of paper. He's calling to the one above, "Would you like to read a few of my poems?" The caption underneath reads: "Poetry is a tough dollar." Regardless of how passionate you feel about poetry, don't quit your day job. Poetry IS a tough dollar.

Some of you will go on to write many poems about many things in your life. You will share your poems with those around you, you'll enter other contests, you'll send your poems off to magazines and a fair number of you will have some poems published.

Regardless of whether you become a prolific poet, or just experiment with the art from time to time, I hope you will recognize if you have a gift for poetry—either reading it, hearing it, or writing it.

Katherine Anne Porter, a native Texan and a novelist and short story writer, said, "One of the marks of having a gift is the courage to use it."

So if you're a "poetry-type person," whether you feel you are a full-fledged poet or not, I hope you will lead, what I call, the poem life. That is, I hope you'll honor your liking for poetry, and that you will let yourself honor the imaginative life in the ways I'm about to outline.

People following their gifts of poetic imagination are always heads-up. They are leading the discovering life, following an intentional mind set and practice that causes them to be living a whole rich life. They're keen observers of everything all about them, as well as their own lives. They take in a great deal of information all the time and they allow themselves to see things differently. They ask themselves if trees and chairs might not have souls; if dogs, like people, speak in many different languages and are mutually intelligible. They see beyond the slick veneers and into the spirit of the world. They ask questions; they read books; they seek to interpret their existence.

And then, deep-down poetic souls observe the rhythms of life. They contemplate the pounding ocean, sunrises and sunsets, blackbirds gathering by the millions during migration. They observe when the mesquite flowers, when it bears fruit, when it loses its leaves. And they seek to comprehend how they fit in with the rhythms of the earth.

The wonder is

how a tree scribbles on the sky
how the sky plagiarizes
without shame
how the earth turns
page after page of grass
and we know this to be
the only handwriting on the wall
~Jan Seale

It's important that people with poetry gifts understand the power of words. They know that the old saying, "Sticks and stones may break my bones but words can never hurt me," is false, that words can hurt and hurt as deeply as any instrument of injury. And they know that words, in their power, have the ability to heal, and to thrill, and to cause laughter, and to impart all kinds of subtleties that enhance our human existence.

People who are engaged in poetry in some way recognize the chiming of events in life, the rhymes, if you will, of living. They see how this thing fits into that. They look for connection and intention. They actively seek what the universe may be extending to them. And they're often delighted by the synchronous behavior of the events in their lives, in the same way their ears are delighted by a song's rhyming lyrics.

Writing poems will make you think more deeply. It will make you strong in individuality. It will cause you to look at your world and at ideas that occur to you as possibilities of new ways to express things. Others around you will begin to value your vision. You will be fulfilling a need in your mind and heart. You will be exercising your love of words and your sense of rhythm and perhaps rhyme. You will be speaking in your native artistic tongue.

I hope, whether you're a hard-core poet, or a poetry lover, or a person with a keen imagination, that above all, you will have the courage to use your gift. I guarantee you, that if you will incorporate poetry in some or all these ways we have talked about, you will never be sorry.

Co-founder's Statement

I am about to commit the unthinkable, speak the taboo words: I don't understand much of the poetry I see published today.

There. It's out. You're free to marvel at my witlessness and put down *riverSedge*, or read on and hear me out.

Let me describe the poem incomprehensible to me. The title is like a neon sign flashing before a church—inappropriate but eye-catching. The poem itself begins in stabs and starts, an initial lyrical fit in bad Thomas/Hopkins designed to show the poet as a gifted but troubled being. It then proceeds without punctuation, becoming a game with the reader determining if a word serves as a complement to the last verb or subject to the upcoming one, and guessing just why certain words free-float at some distance from the body of the poem.

If there are sentences, they are often periodic, with the last word delayed to the first of the following line. The regularity of the affectation is as exciting as a case of hiccups. Along the way, the reader is assaulted by mixed metaphors, bizarre and dissociative images, whims of mind awaiting inspiration. If the poet cannot achieve in words what Dali does in paint, it's obviously the reader's fault for not understanding.

Before the poem ends, there is at least one dream the poet has experienced. What does it matter if it's corny, pat, hyper-subjective, illogical, hallucinatory, or nauseous? It's a dream; it belongs in a poem.

The ending of the poem I can't understand is a retreat. It drifts into the bushes, slips off like Sandburg's foggy cat, tries one last time to confuse or disappoint the reader. In that at least the poem is successful.

So what am I asking for besides strange looks when I say I simply do not understand many of the poems being published today? I'm asking for fewer of them. And in their place, poems with titles like comforting porch lights. Poems with enough punctuation and typographical guidance to free the reader of irritating grammatical exercises. Poems where tone and idea have a contractual marriage. Poems which do not damn themselves with faint praise by "a good line" every now and then (meaning one we can finally understand) but distinguish themselves by clarity and aptness, line after line. Poems which end in revelation, or at least do not dwindle to predictable anti-endings of yawns and shrugs. Poems which are finished pieces, not asking the reader to accompany the poet on some tedious and obscure on-the-site inspection deep inside the poet's cranium.

Surely, Archibald MacLeish never meant his famous statement to set "meaning" in antipathy with "being." The two aren't mutually exclusive. A poem should certainly "be," but just as certainly "mean."

Co-founder's Remarks: Introduction to the first volume re-establishing the journal *riverSedge*

It was 1977 and I was bent over a lighted work desk. I had just separated a long roll of fine photographic paper into sections containing blocks of type, chunks of words comprising poems and essays. When the waxer was hot enough, I rolled it over the backs of these and, squinting carefully, positioned them over the faint blue lines of the matrix page and pressed down. I was preparing *riverSedge* magazine for printing in the Pan American University print shop.

Today that process seems downright quaint. Yet the end result, a 5" X 8" staple-bound volume of 38 pages, was the beginning of a tradition that has endured for the last 37 years. The technology has changed but the need remains.

The literary magazine is a staple of American culture. At last count, there were more than 4,000 of them crisscrossing the land by mail, as well as several hundred in cyberspace. These magazines feature writing by both novices and experienced writers. For the beginning writer, having a poem or story in one of these "little mags" may be all the boost needed to keep on with the fragile work of writing. For the more experienced writer, the mail that comes with a journal containing his or her work breaks up the solitude of the writing room and connects the writer to others publishing alongside. Eventually, a list of first publication credits in literary magazines shows a book editor that the writer being considered has already been vetted by other creditable readers.

I was not alone in my work on the nascent *riverSedge*. The true birth mother was Dorey Schmidt, a teacher in the English Department with me, along with another instructor, Ted Daniels. The fourth was Brian Robertson, an employee at a local museum. We were all writers. As I recall, we advertised through the Texas Association of Creative Writing Teachers newsletter and by word of mouth. And we did a daring thing for the times: we deemed it important to have visuals, art work that would both stand alone and complement the written word. Fortunately, there were some fine local line-drawing artists, as well as photographers.

The work was a way for the four of us, isolated geographically far south of other writers in the huge state of Texas, to connect with like-minded souls, both academic and independent writers and readers. To write is one thing, to edit, another, and in the latter activity, we gathered the writing and art of our artful acquaintances and those strangers who submitted and found us willing, even excited, to further their work. Editing a literary magazine posed a mix of altruism, duty, and, let's face it, a thrill at exercising informed judgment on poems, fiction, and essays. Added to that was the fact that this job was a line item in our resumes as well as being downright fun.

With the renewal of *riverSedge*, I feel again gratitude for the chance to have helped establish and edit a magazine that to this day enjoys a good name. Although there were many years when I watched *riverSedge* being produced and was not a part of that process, still now I see myself as an ancestor, a proud relative of an idea that has had staying power.

Through the intervening years, after the four of us editors left for other endeavors, we watched the metamorphosis of *riverSedge*, often well tended and with much polish by subsequent editors who took up the task, and at other times an orphan, moved here and there in boxes, never quite dying but certainly in hibernation (to mix my metaphors). I am very happy to see a well-organized effort to make *riverSedge* robust again. And I can say with assurance that my writing colleagues over the state and beyond, who have often questioned me about *riverSedge*'s health, are cheered by the prospect.

Every artist should do something for other artists. It's a great corrective to the ego that threatens to consume writers in their peculiar need to share what they know with the world. The editorial ranks of literary magazines are filled with writers and artists who give of their time, most often without monetary compensation, to bring to life artistic work in a venue other than

128

books. Editing is a daunting task, but it's also a kindness to one's profession. Personally, I think every writer should take a due turn as officer of a writers' group, adjudicator for a writing contest, and/or editor of a publication.

And with this unselfishness comes enhancement to the writer/editor's own life. Receiving the work of others and considering it offers a rich matrix for an editor—reading, being in contact with other writers, feeling the triumph or disappointment of submitters, understanding the mindset and the challenges of the editor who might be judging one's own work for another magazine.

So what do I wish for the new *riverSedge*? A delightful gathering of words and art, with all the technologies of modern printing exploited, perhaps with theme issues if time and the publishing process allow. A definite set of values and standards, ethical and literary. An active solicitation of work and clear submission directives which ensure that the editors do not become overwhelmed. A kind and ever helpful approach to accepting and rejecting manuscripts. An intern program that uses the abundance of creative writing students now in our area, stressing the importance of proficiencies in editing. A set of keen-eyed proofreaders who don't allow a single misspelling, misuse, or mispunctuation to spoil the reader's trust in the written page. A robust public image among both writers and readers. Support from the university and from the community. Above all, I would like the new *riverSedge* to have a definite personality, distinguishing itself by whatever characteristics—regional, literary, style, tone, appearance—that the editors agree upon and put forward.

riverSedge was our natural-born child 37 years ago. It's been through a number of caring foster homes. I'm hoping the latest iteration of this worthy child will represent a permanent adoption. Hello, 2014 *riverSedge*!

Remarks on the Occasion of the 40th Anniversary of *riverSedge* October 12, 2017

I remember from 40 years ago the editorial discussions about the name of our journal. Dorey Schmidt, one of our editors and really, the birth mother, thought it up. It had two meanings, depending on where you decided to pause within the word. One readily apparent meaning was—beside the river, on the bank of the Rio Grande. So the "S" in the middle was the possessive of river. This journal was coming from the banks of the Rio Grande. So, it was at "river's edge."

The other meaning was a compound noun: river sedge. The sedge is a grasslike plant, the blades of which are angled, sharp, and distinctive. In other words, sedge has a cutting edge. Because it chooses to grow in or near water, the sedge is always strong, brightly colored, noticeable. It's distinct from common grasses.

With a house full of poets, writers and readers, I don't think I need to belabor the symbolism of the name. Let's just pause on it for a moment: *riverSedge* journal originates on the southern end of a mighty river, and *riverSedge* is colorful, strong, and sharp.

It was amazing how fast *riverSedge*'s reputation grew. Within the first year of our quarterly issues, writers from over the state and beyond began to inquire about *riverSedge*. How was it doing? What sorts of things did we want? Could they submit? As I recall, we enjoyed the growing reputation of *riverSedge*, and especially the connections we made with the submitters. When we found a match between a piece of art and a story or poem, we were delighted.

We did the physical work of publishing as well—first taking the selections to the typesetter at the print shop across Sugar Road, and returning to proof the type. Next we cut out the pieces like paper dolls from the long scrolls on which the typesetting machine spit them out. Standing over a light board, we aligned and glued the type on individual pages especially prepared with grids. Now we made a mock-up of the book, figuring out what went logically with what. Next we positioned the pages by a formula on to a much larger paper—some 16 pages of the book—front and back—per one page of the large sheets, known as signatures. Only then did we turn our precious work over to the print shop manager and his pressmen, who photographed them to the negative, then burned the plates and mounted the plates on the offset press, which printed them front and back. The university print shop was very proud to be able to do this—a first for them—and they would often let us in the press room where we stood while the beautiful paper —special ordered for *riverSedge*—was loaded and watched as *riverSedge* fell into the arms of the letterpress printer and was spit out page by huge page, these to be folded in their intricate pattern, the cover applied, and all the sides trimmed to open up the folds. Finally, a worker stood over a small piece of machinery, which looked like a saddle, laid the creased book pages across it and applied the staples, thus known as a binding that was saddle-stitched—a much more glamorous name than "stapled."

When the issue was ready, boxes were delivered to our office and we went to work mailing complimentary copies to our contributors and encouraging them to share with others. That was *riverSedge* in its infancy and youth. Today's fully realized adult *riverSedge* is quite remarkable—for several reasons:

1) Resurrection in our society is a rare thing. To find a relic, probe its viability, apply emergency measures, and make it like new—that's what happened to *riverSedge*;

2) Another reason for celebration: *riverSedge*'s reputation has miraculously remained through the years of past iterations and inactivity—until the present saviors came along;

3) That it was, and is, one of the most physically attractive journals around, and I don't need to elaborate on the differences in printing processes;

4) Remarkable in that the editors have worked to extend its scope—with plays, reviews and interviews;

5) To produce it still takes hard work, with little or no direct compensation for the editors.

It's important for the writers here at UT-RGV to support and love and help produce *riverSedge*. If you are one of the editors, good for you. It's my feeling that every writer needs to take a turn at other aspects of writing and publishing, serve their time, donate their skills to an art that needs all the help it can get. It doesn't lessen one's creativity to work on the editing, publishing, or technical side of the literary world. Conversely, it actually helps your own writing to know what's going on behind the scenes of the publications you are submitting to. It also helps you feel a part of a huge community of writers. So, if you're local, become involved in helping out *riverSedge*.

As *riverSedge* goes into middle age, here's what I wish for it:

I wish for *riverSedge* high standards for accepting work, and for editing it, both content and form;

I wish *riverSedge* to continue incorporating wide diversity;

I wish *riverSedge* to follow through after the publishing with good marketing strategies;

I wish *riverSedge* to emphasize helpful dialogs with submitters and contributors.

And finally, I wish for the *riverSedge* we founded 40 years ago to keep its unique position geographically and to champion eloquent and worthy writing from across Texas, across the United States, and beyond.

Published in *Scribe* (Writers' League of Texas), volume 27

Institutionalize Yourself

The sharks circle their tank, the turtles loll, the crabs scrunch. Across the hall, I am teaching a writing class. We creatures are co-existing at the marine science laboratory near the tip of South Padre Island. I'm no ichthyologist, so what am I doing here?

I visited the fish one day, saw an empty classroom, and learned from the director that he'd like to increase the public's awareness of the facility. Combine that with a large Winter Texan contingent, and Voila! I have a weekly class of twenty eager memoirists.

Writers with flexible schedules, popular subjects, and a bit of hustle might consider the perks of teaming up with public entities. Waiting out there are museums, churches, centers, parks and libraries that need you. And presumably you could use the exposure and income.

Match your talents to the appropriate market, and further refine. If you've learned the skill of writing personal experience pieces, can you teach it? A special group will welcome you at a senior center or mobile home park.

A birdwatcher? Approach your local nature center about writing trail scripts.

A poet? Check out the Sunday paper for club news, then call the president to suggest a free program of your poems on women, or fishing, or parenting—with the understanding that you will have the privilege of offering your books for sale.

Think outside the box, but always with mutual advantages for you and the institution. Eager to show community involvement, your bank may sponsor a classy lobby signing for you. Or your church might welcome the weekday traffic your class or tutoring service will bring.

Some residential living centers welcome outside teachers and performers. Once I contracted to teach classes in a retirement center through their marketing division, which wanted to entice townspeople to buy apartments there.

Be alert to opportunities to team up with an institution or business for celebrations and holidays. One poet programmed himself into a hobby store to compose original Valentine poems for crafters. A three-day Christmas shopping bazaar in our area annually invites a local writer to grace its huge marketplace.

Although many locations are delighted that you will come to them, and will allow you to charge a fee for your services, others, such as public libraries, have restrictions about money-making on their premises. Don't automatically exclude these from your quest. Acknowledging your energy to present a free program, they may allow you to distribute bookmarks, brochures, and website information.

Independent bookstores and certain national chains have inviting policies about their in-store readings. Sometimes writers may advertise their events, set them up in their store, and take the complete proceeds. These places covet a friendly local-community image, plus the dollars your friends may spend on other books.

Author visits to schools have plummeted due to testing requirements, but there's always a need for child-friendly creative writing teachers in the community. Direct your intent to boys' and girls' clubs, museum outreach, and summer recreation programs. Even if you don't get paid, you have the chance to gain insight into children's perspectives.

When you land a job with an institution, quickly fulfill their requests for publicity material. As the time approaches, check that your agreement is intact. When the event arrives, be early and expect surprises—a strange furniture arrangement, a change in personnel, or—best of all—more attendees than anticipated. It could happen.

You're a writer. Think creatively how to use your words to institutionalize yourself. Your public is calling.

First published as "Craft a Title That Beckons" in *Writer's Digest*, May 2003; reprinted as "Craft a Welcoming Title" in *Start Writing Now*, April 2004

Porch Light Titles

If we're having visitors in the evening, we turn on our porch light. It illumines the entryway, welcoming and guiding our guests as well as helping us identify them upon their arrival. So it is with effective titles.

They are beacons asking readers to come in and be welcome to our stories and poems. They give just enough light for identification and safety, not weak faulty signals nor blinding floodlights. A well-chosen title is a commitment to enlighten and entertain your reader-guest.

Choosing a useful title for a piece of writing often stymies the writer. If one doesn't fortuitously appear, the tired artist may be tempted to give up and assign the first words that present themselves. Perhaps it doesn't really matter.

Au contraire. A fine title, one that is beckoning and illumines what's in store, constitutes an important decision for the writer.

Picking a good title depends a great deal on what you are naming. If it's an instructional piece, you want to find a word or phrase that shows the reader what might be learned in the article. No trickiness, no obscurity, just a clear 150-watt porch light beckoning the reader to come in and get smarter. Of course, cleverness is always welcome.

It's hard to keep how-to titles short because they bear the gist of the whole piece. A title that doesn't explain itself in two or three words usually ends up with a long subtitle.

Choosing a header for other non-fiction, fiction or a poem allows more leeway. Here the intent may be to lure the reader by a teasing metaphor or mystery.

In a short story named "Spider Lilies," my main character is a lonely old woman who hybridizes spider lilies in her yard. But her gardening is not a major component of the plot. Instead, the story reveals the character of the woman herself as both a "spider" and a "lily." A real thing in the story functions as a metaphor and also a title.

Many short story writers use a brief title like John Updike's "Son" or Ring Lardner's "Haircut." These generic-sounding headers don't seem to put off editors or readers. Neither do they mean much when the reader first tries out the page. But upon reflection after the reading, the reader experiences a click of recognition, an "Ah-ha!" moment. The title, and the story, have done their job. So if you title a work "Sisters" or "The Bath" or "Making Love," be sure the title is important to the theme.

You may also emphasize a theme by using a title taken from a phrase in a well-known literary work. Flannery O'Connor's short story title "Why Do the Heathen Rage?" echoes Psalm 2:1. Robert Flynn's "The Midnight Clear" rings with the first line of the Christmas carol "It Came Upon a Midnight Clear."

Often, I find a title for a story embedded in the text. It seems to beckon me to lift it out, set it above the rest of the words as a foreshadowing or an encapsulation of the theme. The title "After Long Silence" came out of a quoted letter in a story about three cousins meeting for the first time as adults. As we edit our stories over and over, we are struck by the truth or aptness of a word or phrase. It's up to us to listen to our writerly selves and take the hint.

Long phrases or whole sentences are sometimes used for short story titles. Joyce Carol Oates's "Will You Always Love Me?" contains a chilling irony while Jessamyn West's"The Mysteries of Life in an Orderly Manner" is purposely vague and grand.

Though true to some extent of all titles, poem titles must certainly mean, not merely be. Because of the heightened use of words in poems, it's imperative that headers for poems be as carefully assigned as any other word in the poem. Often, the word or words used for a poem title are not mentioned at all in the poem body. The title gives powerful clues as to the poem's meaning, or it adds an additional twist to the controlling metaphor of the poem.

Occasionally, a poem title may be used as the first line of a poem, such as:

The Business Boys of Reynosa [title]

are constant as grass,   [text]
own elbows and knees of earth,
invent a new brown for eyes . . .

Used sparingly, so that it doesn't become a cliché in your writing, letting the title function grammatically as the first line of the poem is an effective way to draw the reader in, especially to a poem that catalogs the subject, as this one does.

It doesn't pay to fret over a novel's title because the final title is often at the discretion of the publisher. Still, expending a little thought on a title is prudent. An acquaintance reported the other day that she had finished her book and was shopping it with the working title *From Life*. When an editor or agent opens the manuscript, will the blandness of this header give a weak signal? Probably.

Novel titles are often drawn from well-known literary works. Robert Penn Warren's *World Enough and Time* is taken from a line in the poem "To His Coy Mistress" by the 17th-century poet Andrew Marvell. Hemingway's *For Whom the Bell Tolls* echoes the voice of the earlier poet John Donne.

Some writers keep a running list of titles they might use, such as "Compromising Positions," "The Importance of Shade," "Roaches," "Incident Command," and "Prior Commitments." They note down words and phrases that strike them as apt or interesting. They may draw on this list when they need a title. Or, on a dry day, they will use it to ply their imagination and trigger new ideas.

Title your work in such a way that recalling the subject of your writing will not be a major problem. If you're forgetful or have a large output, choose titles that give you clues as to what the piece is about. Otherwise, you may be sitting before your files list puzzled about what is what.

Laziness advertises itself in titles like "Thoughts on Love," "Life," "One Day," "Time Stood Still," or "Hope." True, you may see any of these examples on published writings by prominent writers.

But reading the work itself, one can usually determine how the author intentionally uses the bland title for a special effect.

Just when you think you've found the perfect title, there it is, already used, heading up a magazine article or flashing from an airport paperback stand.

With all of us using a common set of words, duplications are bound to occur from time to time. There's no need to research a poem or short story title to avoid duplication; for common titles, these are inevitable, and except for copying famous short story titles, generally accepted. But for a proposed book title, do snoop around in *Books in Print* to see if you've inadvertently assigned your book manuscript with a name already used. If so, choose another.

If you still have trouble relinquishing your original title, see if you can vary it a little, keeping certain key words. For example, if you see *The Time of Her Life* already used, try *Times She Chose to Call Her Own*. Often the better title comes from the author's veering away from duplicating another.

Finally, keep in mind when you're titling a work that too many words may create a nightmare for the text designer of literary magazines or anthologies, especially those in a 5" X 8" format. Reasonable length in titles becomes crucial. If two poems are being considered equally for publication, the poem with the extremely long title is likely to lose out. If your work with the long title is chosen, your title may have to be shortened to accommodate limited space on a table of contents page or for text page design.

A good title, like a useful porch light, illumines the way home. Carefully choose and polish the light that you want your readers to receive a signal from. Home, in the case of your writing, is meaning.

A version given at Texas Council of Teachers of English Language Arts 2014 state meeting, Corpus Christi, Texas and published in *English in Texas*, 2014

Creative Joy: Process And Product

My junior high teaching job came up suddenly when a family move left me unemployed. On the spur of the moment, I was hired to teach eighth grade language arts in a time when classes were heavily ability-grouped. There were twelve ability-grouped classes in language arts in this junior high, with the 801's as the best. You can probably guess what the latest hire was assigned—the 812's.

My class was a mixture of those whose parents refused to let them be in a special-ed class, brand-new monolingual-in-Spanish immigrants from Mexico, and older teenagers who had regularly been taken out of school to follow the crops.

There were hardly any materials, just one workbook for grammar. The supervisor for language arts was as bewildered as I was about what to do with this group. I soon put the workbooks in the corner and began to improvise.

As primitive as this may sound, I finagled old filmstrips from the librarian, took them home and dipped them in bleach to get rid of the images, and brought them back to the classroom where the students drew pictures and words on them. We then ran the strips through a hand-cranked projector for a program of sorts.

But the most successful project was writing and producing a school newspaper. They really got into this. My one requirement was that all the copy had to be in English. The boys drew fabulous pictures of motorcycles and labeled the parts. The girls collected dedications of songs from the student body. Some furnished recipes. I still have my recipe from Elva, a thoughtful girl bussed in every day from the King Ranch. It's titled "How to cook a cow's head in a pit."

There were also essays. Robert wrote a narrative about getting into trouble with his father and then getting out of it again.

Because he had a flair for the narrative and was one of my best writers, I sought to correct one of Robert's sentences by putting in the margin the comment "Awkward, try this again." When Robert received his marked paper, he waited patiently beside my desk to talk to me. I still remember how he leaned down with his paper in hand and said quietly and very respectfully, "Miss, my name is not Awkward. My name is Robert."

Well, the newspaper was a great hit. They sold it for a nickel at lunch time and had lots of sales, mainly because we had no door on our classroom and the lunch line queued up outside my room at the period when my 812's met. That was long ago, and still in my memory are the names and faces of those students—struggling, trying hard, hopefully learning some English, and teaching me as well. They were perhaps my greatest teaching challenge and whatever they learned, bunched together as they were, they learned through the practice of creativity.

* * *

All creators go through six stages of creativity, whether they are inventors, scientists, entrepreneurs, educators, writers, or artists. You can apply these stages in your classroom as well as in your personal life.

Stage One in the creative process can be seen as the Aha! moment. A creation is born in at least two different ways. In the purposefully directed instance, the idea comes from the outside, such as when you give your students a project or assignment. In that case, there's an initial idea presented and how it will be implemented is the excitement, the discovery of Stage One. In the improvisationally directed, the would-be creator "thinks up" the idea. The person has some kind of innate urge to combine certain things, or express an idea. Here the idea comes initially from the student, possibly prompted by some subject being considered in the classroom.

The creative act may be a beautiful artistic thing, or on a more everyday level, it may come from a problem that needs solving, filling some deficiency, or meeting a challenge. Either way, Stage One, the Aha! moment, is important to the whole process.

In the best lesson plans, there will be both purposefully directed and improvisationally directed assignments. Sometimes creative projects need limiting; otherwise, they will just spin off into chaos. With other assignments, it's important to allow the student to run with his or her Aha! moment—even if the product from this kind of assignment will be harder to evaluate. Here is where your wisdom and genius as a teacher will kick in. Thinking through your assignments, you decide how much you want to influence a creative assignment.

Stage Two, the Easy-Does-It time, is the first period of real work on a creative project. It is usually fast, with more questions, leading to some research, which in turn produces more questions. Insights may come quickly, with options piling up. There's often a feeling of euphoria. "Isn't this fun! I'm succeeding! It will happen!" If the project is for a group, you have no doubt observed Stage Two in your students when they gather in groups. There's often crackling excitement, a couple of students jumping up and down with the adrenalin of ideas, a struggle to get organized, to pick a leader.

Stage Three, a second period of work, might be dubbed the Hanging-in-There time. Here willpower has to kick in. There's deeper inquiry, with harder questions. How will this be different from what's already been done? How will the story end? What is the focus of the poem? Organization begins in earnest. Willpower has been called the greatest human strength, and in this third stage of creative effort, its presence will determine whether the project comes to fruition.

Stage Four is the Stumped period. Lucky is the person or group with a creative project who has not encountered a time of difficulty in succeeding. The premise may seem doubtful, the timing wrong, the materials unavailable. For the writer, the heroine of the story in progress begins to act out, or there is no rhyming word available to match up with another at a crucial place in the poem. Perhaps for the first time, you as a teacher may have to step in to a group project. Tempted as you may be to offer an instant solution, it's wise to let the problem or difficulty bubble for a while. Your role is to encourage alternatives, problem-solving, and cooperation. Sooner or later, the creative problem will yield to solution. The main ingredients here are courage and patience, along with keeping the project in mind so the subconscious can work and the conscious mind can recognize solutions.

As for the Stumped phase in individual creators, I want to interject an interesting consideration here. At about ten years of age, the corpus callosum, which is the rope-like bundle of neural tissue between the left and right brain segments, finally becomes fully functional. It facilitates communication between the right and left brain hemispheres.(The "soft-spot" on babies' heads is the declivity left for the corpus callosum to fill up.) When the right and left brain hemispheres are fully connected, the left brain, with its logical, rational, judgmental thinking begins to exercise influence over the right brain.

Up until this time the right brain has enjoyed a period of invention, fantasy, and imagination—with very pleasurable creativity. We see evidence in the wild freedom of young children when they play or when they work on an art project. Now, at about fourth grade, the left brain may tell the right brain that the picture being drawn is awful, that the story being written is dumb, that the game invented is stupid. A wise teacher will notice when a child repeatedly starts over, wadding up the drawing or the story and tossing it in the wastebasket. Just going over the six steps of creating something in a simplified way, pausing to emphasize the Stumped period, is often enough to help the child see what's happening and move past it. Those children who can overcome the heavy left-brain emphasis on order, judgment, competition, winning, and doing things to please others will retain the ability to move on out to a life of enjoyment as creative people.

Stage Five, the Eureka! moment, sometimes described as the Hallelujah! moment, is the moment that not only artistic creators are seeking but also those in major research in such fields as science, medicine, business, social work, and education. Not consistently, but sometimes the break-through to being stumped in Stage Four will come at an unexpected moment, when it seems the mind is resting or preoccupied with other things. "Chance favors the prepared mind," Louis Pasteur wisely observed. The Eureka moment often comes during sleep or when reading unrelated material. Einstein had a break-through one day with his theory of relativity when he was simply observing a passing train. Descartes is said to have produced Cartesian geometry by observing the movements of a fly on the wall of his bedroom. And we have Percy Spencer, a military engineer, to thank for the microwave, brought about when he was working on a radar set and noticed that a candy bar had melted in his pocket.

Depending on the complexity of the project, it may be that after the Eureka! moment, the creator will return to Stage Two, the first flash of work, and repeat the stages through Stage Five until the project is complete. You can see how this would readily work for writing a novel, where each chapter has to be worked through, with new situations and conflicts figured out.

Stage Six, to put it in a literary term, is the Denouement. It's the mop-up, being faithful in the carry-through, honoring the details. The creator can finally see the light. Sharing the work may be implicit in the finish. Receiving comments may provoke new ideas for future creativity.

As you become aware of the six steps of creativity, practice applying them creatively in your classroom and in your personal and family life. Devise ways to let your students experience the six steps of creativity. Will the creative project be purposefully directed by you, or will you throw the net broadly and let students take it from there? Can you counsel the impatient and the discouraged to see a work through? Can you help a child or a group salvage a wrong turn and learn from it?

At every step, emphasize the pleasure of creating. Process is so important. Devise as many ways as possible to help kids love the process. If a student learns to take pleasure in the "doing," such character traits as patience, happiness, and self-control will be forming. When I asked a writer to comment on creative structure in his home as he was growing up, he said, "Oh, I don't know. We all just did whatever was fun for us."

Our educational system is geared toward results, and of course, those are important. But we need to keep always in mind that the student is living a life now, as a fully-entitled human being, not just as a preliminary form of human life that must be changed, molded, trained, prepared and filled. So we show our students that what they did today on their project was satisfying in itself; we ask them to notice the fun of it, to realize that creating is a special human gift available to us all. Sometimes the process is hard, the work arduous, but in the end we should all feel better for having entered into creativity.

Avoid distinctions between "creative" and "not-creative." Someone said, "Trying to pin down creativity is like trying to nail Jello to the wall." Creators in the arts are often singled out as the only creative people in our midst. Others say, "Oh, I'm not creative."

But everyone is born with creativity. It may not be the creativity of the arts, or of performance. Yet we all, each one of us, live our daily lives on a layer of universal creativity—every piece of clothing, kitchen gadget, fixture, piece of furniture, communication item, and means of transportation had to be invented, created by someone. We don't doubt the creativity of millions of people unknown personally to us.

And we shouldn't doubt our own because creativity is a component of human nature, whether it's used for "high art" or for getting along in our everyday world.

Cake mixes first came on the market in the 1930s and they did fairly well, but in the 1950s there was a slump. What had gone wrong? Contrary to the myth that women wanted to add eggs and other ingredients so they could feel more creative, what really saved cake mixes was the invention of canned frostings. Women wanted to decorate their plain cake-mix cakes. They pored over magazine directions for making medieval castles, football fields, and three-ring circuses and the cake mix was saved from extinction.

* * *

Creativity bids us to see things in a new way, that is, to go beyond the information given, recombining, thinking in unconventional ways, using little known or neglected means. To be clinical, it starts in the frontal lobe, that part of the brain which has the boundless capacity to dream up things. Feeding our own creativity both in the classroom and away from it makes us happier people and better teachers. Creating alongside our students gives them powerful examples when they see we are unafraid to write a quatrain or a sonnet and furthermore that we are enjoying the process.

Our own personal bliss is enhanced when we make something. A commercial artist, defining the pleasure of creativity, noted it as:

> that soul-filling feeling that you get when creativity is really flowing. Sometimes you get it gardening, or painting, or decorating for Christmas. It's that pure fun feeling when you're making something out of nothing. It's just coming out of you with no resistance.

Albert Einstein gave a challenge to parents and teachers. "It is the supreme art of the teacher to awaken joy in creative expression and knowledge." There is nothing quite like the high of being "in flow." Time passes without notice. Life goes on around. The passion of creation takes center stage. The fun of it buoys one along.

Catching the brightness, the soulfulness, the sheer happiness of making art is of inestimable value to any human. For the young, it may be enough to inform a lifetime.

Creating is finding the sweet spot.

Part Four: Journaling

I always say, Keep a diary and someday it'll keep you.

~Mae West

Recollecting in Tranquility

I can't imagine the life of a writer without a place for ideas, happenings, rants, musings, confessions, lists—any of which might possibly be utilized in a piece of writing. For as far back as I can remember, I have kept journals. Robert Moss, a prolific Australian writer has observed, "You don't have to be a writer to be a journaler, but journal keeping will make you a writer anyway."

It seems writers are practically born talking to themselves. They are plagued by a running script in their heads, a story line they can't escape. "She's walking into the room and picking up a book." In my long life of talking to myself, I have tended journals on different subjects. There's the big general one where observations about life, including writing, reads some days like a dreary five-line diary ("Goals for finishing how-to book: 9 weeks to Christmas, 20 pages a week, 4 pages a day"), right beside another entry of schoolgirl excitement ("I feel so hyper by the news that my play will be performed"). Turn the page to a pouty list under "Ugly Titles" ("Stories that Go Sour," "Ideas with No Redeemable Value," "Darkest Before the Blackout") and across from that, a tap dance stream of consciousness ("Everything calls—all the fluttering on the clotheslines of life, leaves, tatters of an aged hem, chicken bits, onion chips dragging the soup pot, voices, notes, things in a pocket, looseness, float, drift, scatter, free flight, tumbling, blithery, directional, directionless").

In addition to this main journal, I keep a dream journal, a thankfulness journal, and four grandmother journals, one for each grandchild. (The dream journal is discussed in another essay here). By now, you may be wondering how I have time to live life, what with this plethora of recording. I've never aspired to write in all the journals on a daily basis. The general journal and the dream one get a frequent workout. Let me describe the other two kinds briefly.

The thankfulness journal ascends when I've had enough morning coffee. I pick it up and try for a quick list of 20 things I'm thankful for right then. Dating these lists gains importance for remembering one's frame of mind during a given period. Looking through my thankfulness journal, I note that 22 years ago this month, I was grateful for free grapefruit, a huge flock of parrots overhead, the ability to say no, and for all autonomic body parts.

The grandmother notebooks record my grandsons' sayings and doings when I am with them three or four times a year. Now all teens and beyond, from time to time I trap them and read portions to them. They roll their eyes and squirm—one recently opined that my personal account of him was "kinda boring"—but I intuit they are secretly pleased by the attention. And the one who is grown and married, living in various places around the world, sends me appreciative emails when I copy from his journal an endearing paragraph detailing an antic when he was four or five. He says his wife likes the forecast of what to expect of their children.

I highly recommend the grandparent journal for the points it garners from the busy parents of the children. These beleaguered adults are trying to support their families and be good parents; they have voiced appreciation for my recording specifics they had not had time to do themselves, such as their sons' food preferences, toys, and distinctive reactions to the world. Grandparent journals have the added benefit of safely draining off the darling remarks of one's immediate descendants from conversations with friends who may be bored or jealous.

What makes us want to get down on paper the stuff of our lives? There will always be a partial unknowable answer to this question, a tax-free shoulder shrugging, but other reasons may present themselves more rationally.

One that comes to mind is a bad memory, and I'd better talk about that before I forget it. A good friend commented recently that having a sketchy memory in late life bothered her very little since she had had to put up with a bad memory all her life. That's not the reason we're girlfriends but it certainly does contribute to our compatibility. I know better than to trust that an aha! moment or an account of a significant event will be safe in the storehouse of my mind. I'd better write it down.

Here I will confess to a deviation from neat daybooks. Part of my journal-keeping for help later in writing is notepads all over the house, in my purse, and in the car. These I grab at any time and note only one thing per sheet. When I've collected a handful of them, I sort them and put them in file folders with labels like "Odd people and things," "Flash fiction ideas," and "Poem ideas: birds." This cuts down on the harvesting of ideas when I'm ready to write something I think there's an audience for.

When I was young and in a writing program at the University of Louisville, it was fashionable for those of us in the seminars to carry around an attractive hardback journal which was drawn importantly from backpacks and totes to be utilized when an idea presented itself. Surely there are still these old-fashioned devices for harvesting one's thoughts, but I often wonder if this practice of keeping a real book will be totally subsumed by creative writing students jotting themselves down in "Notes" on their iphones or simply blogging or Facebooking to expunge their excess thought. Not me. I've got to save my mental machinations on a tree-derived page.

Although often used interchangeably, the terms "journal," "diary," and "daybook" connote subtle differences. A diary implies a daily sequence of perfunctory events, a "what I did today." A friend showed me her mother's five-line diary, kept for almost a lifetime. I noticed on one line only a notation: "Charles died today." Charles was the woman's husband of forty years. Okay, she had only one line for that.

The daybook name derives from business, when a log was kept for accounting later on. The definition now includes a more or less chronological approach to informal writing.

A journal sprawls, at times intimate and focused, on other pages factual and random. A journal claims space for leisurely musings, rushes of anger, declamations of ecstasy. It can be as bright and sassy as the keeper pleases, or as piddling and prosaic. It gets written in whenever it's called upon. The very name itself suggests a trip, a journey, a sequencing of emotional and intellectual time. We may fling at it any number of observations as life processes in front of us. All the stuff that goes on around us and in our minds is fair game.

Yesterday, I saw a bird with whiskers, had a meaty conversation, read a quote to die for—these must be preserved. Has there been an unusual conversation on an elevator with a stranger? And will it slip into the street grate of oblivion if I don't record it? I know the answer. The event goes into my journal. I may or may not use it directly in a piece of writing. Maybe I'll simply find it amusing to read later on. Who knows? Not me, at the time I choose to record it.

Journals have saved many a friendship. By that I mean that one can confide in a journal certain life experiences ad nauseum that would damage a friendship in their monotony, controversial theme, or frankness. The very nature of private writing gives an air of secretiveness but allows the journal keeper great freedom to unburden herself.

List-making has achieved prominence in my general journal. There was a time when I had so many distractions and directions in my life there was no way I could actually stop to ponder a concept, a large idea, a major problem. I had deadlines on writing assignments—a family humor column for a newspaper and a cultural watch for a literary journal—plus a fulltime teaching job and a family of five to preside over. I found it handy to keep in my journal running lists of items I intended to write about, these under headings for the newspaper such as "Things I Hate," "Camping Calamities," and "Excuses Children Use" and for the magazine "Reasons We Hafta NAFTA" and "Making Literature Down Among the Sheltering Palms." My journals may be credited with keeping me level-headed, even sane in times of stress.

In my late mother's centenarian years, she held lengthy whispered conversations with herself throughout the day, an act which I found amusing and a bit daft. Now I find it a useful trait that I have appropriated in the form of journal keeping. I close with one fierce conversation I had some years ago, titled "An argument with my journal on the eve of writing a short story":

Me: Get organized! Know everything about the piece before beginning.

Journal: Know that the story lies out there.

Me: But I don't know where to begin.

Journal: Begin anywhere. If you need to, tell yourself this probably isn't the beginning.

Me: Okay, but how would it end? I have to have an ending in mind.

Journal: More than likely, the ending will occur to you as you develop the story. Or, you can always get tired and quit.

Me: First, I have to figure out the point of view.

Journal: Either "I" or choose one of your characters and go for it. Nothing is irreversible in early drafts.

Me: This idea doesn't even have a central theme.

Journal: You are on a road to discovery. No destination if you don't start out.

Me: I haven't struggled, practiced enough.

Journal: There is time before the dark; the best might be yet to be.

Me: I have told all the stories that mean anything to me.

Journal: Oh come now . . . you've told some of the stories that have passed your way.

Me: I won't be able to finish it and then I really will have failed, let myself down.

Journal: You'll have a work in progress. Besides, you hardly ever leave a piece unfinished . . . must be your Virgo nature . . . perfectionism.

Me: I will hurt someone's feelings; they'll recognize themselves.

Journal: Some stories are worth the cost of superficial acquaintances and vain relations.

Me: I'll write it and then have to market it forever.

Journal: Don't be lazy! Marketing is an envelope and a stamp.

[2020: going to the "Submission" page].

Me: The good stuff can't be written.

Journal: Disguise it; go on and write it.

Me: What I write might be a cliché.

Journal: You don't know. If it isn't, you were wrong to think it.

Me: I need to straighten my desk, clear up all my paperwork before starting.

Journal: That, my friend, you know very well is not going to happen. An unrealistic human condition.

Me: The subjects I think about to write on, I'm not sure will 'work' anymore.

Journal: What else could you write on?

Me: Maybe I can't get it published and my time will be wasted.

Journal: Publication is not the best reason for writing. Just say it's a compulsion. Oh, and a kind of superior game of solitaire.

Me: What if I get stuck? Maybe I can't finish.

Journal: Go do something else for a while—but only for a short while.

***

As I recall, my journal won and I went on to write the short story.

Such Stuff as Dreams are Made Of

Lately I have been reading through my dream journals of thirty years, looking for some justification for having kept these accounts of my soul's night wanderings for this long a time. Early on, I tried to keep my dream accounts without so much as an exclamation point by way of emotional reaction to them. Then a psychic suggested a new way. Now I record the dream as fast as possible—it's a great way for a writer to start the day—then draw two sturdy horizontal lines and write an interpretation. Sometimes I don't think there is one, but as soon as I begin to whine to that effect, the meaning comes slamming down on me. "Oh! The road with huge ruts means I'm in a rut . . . no, two ruts."

If I've had several dreams, I write key words in the margin—tip-offs to remind myself what they were about. Otherwise, I'll get so wrapped up in recording one that the others may fall into that nearby abyss of forgetfulness.

Reading through the dated journals, I see that the dreams somewhat match my waking activities. When I was teaching, I spent many frustrating hours at night trying to find the right room in a building, or realizing that I was charged with teaching a certain course and had never shown up for it. Sometimes I'd get to the class and have nothing to say.

During the childbearing years, I often had visions of rocking, cajoling, cooking, and chauffeuring. That was the period where I dreamed repeatedly that I gave birth to a frozen chicken! My grown sons tell me this was not a flattering dream.

Becoming a grandmother of four grandsons, my dreams have often featured little boys. These children need rescuing and protecting. Sometimes they make wise precocious pronouncements. Rather belatedly, and redemptive of the frozen chicken dream, these children are named not their real names but the names of their fathers—my sons.

The loss of relatives and friends precipitates both sad and exhilarating dreams. I never tell my friends if an ill fate befalls them in my night. On the other hand, I'm eager to share with others if a deceased parent or beloved friend visited me in dreamland, complete with eye contact and voice inflection. These encounters are so very real. They are of the type Alexander Pope commented on when he said, "You eat, in dreams, the custard of the day."

The last few years, conferences and campgrounds dominate my dreams. There are endless workshops, outings, dorms, groups. I travel to these on busses and trains and in cars that often break down on country roads or in sinister valleys. When I finally arrive, I'm bewildered by a huge campus, or the tent is drafty, or it's raining on the campground.

Certain themes have prevailed throughout the thirty years. Buildings seem to fascinate me: I experience vast rooms, staircases, arches, hidey holes, hallways. In their gardens are levels up and down, pathways, ledges. I take comfort in these dreams because they are of the ilk of Jung's famous dream of a house with various rooms, a dream which helped inspire his theory of the collective unconscious in which we draw in our sleep from a cultural storehouse of archetypes.

Church happenings loom large, no doubt because I was brought up in a Baptist parsonage. Parishioners mostly argue and do inappropriate things in the sanctuary.

And then there are the animals. Fish swim in air, peacocks are peevish, parrots attack, and black and white cows and cats wander by.

The lost purse dreams have been the most persistent theme throughout the decades. These dreams may include a green straw purse (which I've never owned), as well as my flute and briefcase—basically anything with a strap or handle. My friend Rusty has the lost purse dream too, so I addressed this poem to her:

> Your eyes light up. You have it too.
> Sometimes the one you lose
> is cream-colored, cloth.
> Mine is almost always black.

We agree we have spent valuable
REM years on fruitless searches.
The last bad night I had with mine
was on a bus in Mexico. I looked
for it among a million chicken cages,
finally called home without it.

We agree we have wasted
our creative subconscious,
that the dream is 100 percent insecurity,
that we should report to our therapists.
Instead, how about:
if I find your purse in my dream,
I'll return it immediately,
no questions asked?

You do the same,
even if it takes a moving van
and an assistant Scheherazade.

One of the most frustrating things about my dreams is how
weak their plots are. When I was a child, I had good strong
nightmares, waking up in a sweat and running to my mother for
comfort. Chow dogs bit me and robbers jumped out from behind
shadowy shrubbery. During WWII, my pre-school dreams were
about "the draft" getting me, since at the supper table, there was
talk of "the draft" getting a young man, and then in the evening, a
parent would lower the window beside my bed in case there was "a
draft."

In my adult years, the predicaments just crawl along,
needlings after annoyances after irritations, daring the events to
move on decisively and give me a thrill or a shudder. Clothes don't
fit, doors don't close, phones ring and cannot be answered.
Someone bothered me in a dream recently to say I had not been
giving a proper long "e" to "ecological," also that I had not been
using "cellulary" properly. I found the need to call a halt to such
silliness by waking up.

One person I know enjoys laughing at the visions he has
when he is feverish, different from his regular dreams. Coming

down with a cold, he dreams math-related dreams, in which a triangle has to be blue, or two crossed masts on a boat must equal the number 4. My favorite dream in the twilight zone of fever is one in which I was driving a mattress down the street.

The importance of plot may have something to do with why starting or ending a modern novel with a dream is verboten. Editors argue that the reader does not appreciate being tricked initially into a false reality. And who among teachers of creative writing has not gnashed her teeth, after wading through an exciting student narrative, to learn "Then I woke up"?

If I look up a symbol, it's usually the wrong meaning for me. Lately, my dreams have red or yellow objects in them. When I noticed the prevalence, that seemed like a good omen—you know, loud happy colors. But when I looked them up in my dream symbol dictionary, red was only blood and violence, and yellow was indecision. So now I'm trying to dream in green. Maybe purple.

"Trying to" is what's called intentional dreaming. Before you go to sleep, you tell yourself you want to dream an answer, or have a splendid new idea, or solve a messy problem. I haven't quite conquered intentional dreaming yet, maybe because I think there's something disloyal about working the deep unconscious that way. I want my dreams to be vacations for my brain.

Lately, I've been wondering what will become of my dream journals when I die. Perhaps they'll be tossed out, but maybe a family member will be interested. I'm the kind of person who would take a dead relative's journal and read it because, somehow, things like that ought to be done. Off and on now for a while I have been reading the journals of my late husband's Uncle Buddy ("took Mary's blood pressure at 3 p.m.-185 over 95. Way too high but what's to do?").

A few people make a living studying dreams and I'd gladly give my dream diaries over to these folks if they can prove that they're making some headway on the science. One of their theories is that dreams are scraps of reality the brain is trying to make sense of. Freud thought that dreaming was our way to keep our wishes and desires from waking us up.

Nobody keeps a dream journal for thirty years without some intention. Fuzzy-headed and sleep-drunk, I have persisted. I believe that studying my dreams helps me know that certain someone who is at the heart of my being, that personality on my "committee" that is the authentic me.

And I like the proof that there's more to the world than what we can take in sensorially in the light of day, that there's another world over which we have no control. The workings of our minds and souls are still mysteries. Maybe dreams are the realm of the Divine bursting through the dense fog of our everyday humanity. Dogen, a thirteenth–century Japanese Zen monk, thought so: "Who could doubt that a dream is enlightenment, since it is not within the purview of doubt?"

The biggest reason for me to record my dreams may be my sense of play. What better way to begin the day? I like the adventure, happenstance, serendipity, message, even the dark side of dreams, and there seems to be no way to hold on to these except to write them down.

Part Five: Looking at the Light

Should you ask me, whence these stories?
Whence these legends and traditions . . .

~Henry Wadsworth Longfellow

Published in *Concho River Review,* Spring 2014

Tripping the Light Fantastic:
A Look at Texas Poets Laureate

When I was 17 years old and a freshman at Baylor University, the campus newspaper, *The Lariat,* announced a quatrain poetry contest. "Well, why not?" I thought and wrote a modest 19th-century style quatrain:

> Within a solitude there is
> a soundless cavern of delight,
> where thought can play with naked ease,
> and soul can wander out of sight.

Now that I think about it, it was probably the last abstract poem I ever wrote. Still, I took it to the newspaper office and a few days later was notified that I'd won. Whoopee! I went to get my prize. It was a little green book of poetry by the then Texas Poet Laureate, Margaret Royalty Edwards of Waco. I looked at the front page of that book and wondered, "What's a poet laureate?" I was to find out, in an exact way, years later—"and that has made all the difference."

Since 1932, Texas has been nourished by 49 poets laureate, including cowboys, professors, homemakers, dentists, entertainers, lawyers, songwriters—but all poets. I am Number 49, serving the year May 2012 to May 2013. The fact that I name their vocations as other than poets is not a reflection on their craft but a commentary on the fact that poetry has never been a paying proposition. When people ask me if the state pays my way to speaking engagements, I tell them no, that the post is long on honor and short on funds, but our individual hosts are usually generous in paying our transportation, housing, and an honorarium. We make our own arrangements, with very few of us of getting rich from the post.

Still, having no operating funds from the state allows us to interpret the post with great latitude. There are no specific duties, no filing of reports, no accountability. Even at that, most of our Texas poets laureate have put in their year as a time of intense travel, interviews, presentations, and publishing, serving, as you might expect of our dreamy selves, as if we were actually getting paid for it. (By the way, that's the way we say the plural of "poet laureate" since "laureate" is the adjective.)

Two poets laureate are chosen at each biennial Texas Legislature session, one for the current year and one for the following year. Once they are designated, they retain the title for life. Checking with the ten current living poets laureate, we find the majority of them very busy in some form of poetry, with as many engagements as they want or can manage five-six-seven years after their one-year appointments.

If you are doing the math in your head, you have already noted that 1932 to 2013 should have more than 49 poets. In earliest times, the poets were appointed for two-year periods, (one even for three years so as not to disturb the Texas Centennial by a change) and there were a number of shameful years where nobody stepped up to the plate to get the poet laureate nominations organized and put through the Legislature.

Anyone can nominate a person to become Texas poet laureate. Finalists' names come through the Texas Commission on the Arts and are handled by the State Artists' Committee appointed by the governor, lieutenant governor, and speaker of the house. After the selection, the Legislature formally appoints them in a ceremony at the Capitol.

The name "laureate" comes from the Greek "laurel." That's the crown of laurel leaves placed on the heads of the winners at the Olympic games. At some point in time, the laurel crown was used to designate the higher-order thinking arts, not just the shot-put.

Then, in the Middle Ages, the noble households needed a writer for ceremonies such as christenings, birthdays, marriages, and deaths. So a poet laureate was appointed to write appropriate poems for these occasions.

England really glorified the post. Their poets laureate held their posts for life. Alfred, Lord Tennyson was England's only poet laureate for 42 years! The British poets laureate were required to write poems for special occasions, and they were given a pension.

In the United States, we have a "Poet Laureate Consultant in Poetry," formerly called the "Consultant in Poetry, Library of Congress," the name being changed in 1986.

A poet laureate may be appointed for any sort of entity or association. There are poets laureate for cities, counties, regions, and clubs.

But now for some interesting facts about our Texas poets laureate: When Texas poets laureate are mentioned, some folks immediately think of all women, or all men. The truth is that we've had 21 males and 28 females in the post, a moderate distribution.

The post is also associated with that illustrious long-time body, The Poetry Society of Texas. It is true that at first many appointments were made from the influence of the membership of this group. But there have been many appointments, especially in recent years, of non-members.

Before I became poet laureate, I assumed that the poets laureate would invariably be taken from the larger cities. On looking into their hometowns, I was surprised to note that of the 49 so far, only seven were listed as from Dallas—for many years the hub of Texas poetry—although if we counted Denton, McKinney, and Plano—the Dallas area—there would be more. Four are listed from Houston proper—although the same would be true for the numbers in the Houston area as for Dallas. Still there was a respectable number of poets laureate from little towns, like McCamey, Cisco, Vernon, Burkburnett, and from midsize places—Victoria, Wichita Falls, Lubbock, and McAllen.

By the way, I am the first poet laureate from the Rio Grande Valley.

As far as I can tell, the ages of the poets laureate when they were appointed ranged from 43 to 79. Our most recent oldest poet laureate died in the last year, Mildred Baass of Victoria, at the age of 95. There's a wonderful picture of her on the Internet, posing under the Poet Laureate Tree in Granbury with other attending poets during the Langdon Festival of the Arts.

The Poet Laureate Tree is on the property of a couple of arts champions, Dominque and Charles Inge. Each year in September, they sponsor a picnic around the designated Poet Laureate Tree, a large live oak with roots drinking from the nearby Granbury Lake. They have placed a plaque with the names of the poets laureate who have read under it, now totaling ten.

In the early decades, the poets took their cues from the Romantic poets of England in the 19th century. Retrospectively, some of their names seem intentionally poetic, serendipitously alliterative like Dollilee Davis Smith or Grace Noll Crowell, or forecasting their destinies, like Jenny Lind Porter, who was a relative of the famous O'Henry—William Sidney Porter. The critic R.S. Gwynn commented on early Texas female poets, some of them Texas poets laureate as "trinomial poetesses with resonant names."

What of the subject matter of the early poets laureate of Texas? Nature, moral character, and love dominated, often using the formal language of 19th– and early 20th–century poets, with "Thee's", "Thou's", "o'er's," and "twixt's." It may be only a slight exaggeration to say there were almost as many poems on bluebonnets as there were fields of bluebonnets. Idealized weather, with beautiful sunsets, clear skies, and shining moon and stars were ever-present, with an occasional nod to the wind, heat, and drought of Texas. Prayers, longings, and odes echoed the tastes of the times.

Even with the loftiness, the poets' senses of humor often gleamed through the dross. Dollilee Davis Smith, the poet laureate from 1943 to 1945, wrote a quatrain entitled "She Says:"

I used to question, helplessly,
Why man has more success through life,
But have determined this to be
Because a woman has no wife.

Carlos Ashley, Texas Poet Laureate from 1949 to 1951, managed to exist very nicely between the cowboy poets and the intelligentsia. A graduate of TCU, with a law degree, on the state attorney general's staff, and subsequently a state senator, Ashley wrote a volume titled *That Spotted Sow & Other Hill Country Ballads*, which his cousin recently presented me a copy of. Typical of his humor is a poem lamenting the disadvantages of eating sauerkraut. After enumerating various stages of indigestion, Ashley writes a final verse:

> O Lord, behold my withered form;
> Thou knowest all I've been through;
> Have mercy on Thy servant, Lord—
> For God's sake, change the menu.

Though he had access to the highest government halls in Texas, he could cut pretentions readily, in the "Aw shucks" voice of the rural rube. Here's his double quatrain titled "Values:"

> Oh, the glamour and the clamor
> That attend affairs of state
> Seem to fascinate the rabble
> And impress some folks as 'great.'

> But the truth about the matter
> In the scale of loss and gain—
> Not one inauguration's worth
> A good slow two-inch rain.

Grace Noll Crowell was a remarkable laureate. She produced a whopping 27 volumes of poetry. If she were living today, we would say her poems "went viral" as she became known nationally, ironically for her championing the home and housewifery. With a similar sickly nature as Elizabeth Barrett Browning, Crowell was chronically confined to her bed and not able to keep the spick-and-span house she longed to get up and keep for her husband, a writer. Her good friend Beatrice Plumb, writing Crowell's biography, wrote of an incident:

> When her husband found her picking at his typewriter with two uncertain fingers he laughed affectionately, rumpled her black shining hair, and pocketed the poem. He was the writer in that family! Her job was to get rosy and strong again.

But Crowell continued to write from her sickbed and it was not long until she began to sell her poems. Ironically, she extolled the virtues of household work (all the while finding immunity from it) noted here in a poem called "The Homemakers":

> A happy woman singing at her work,
> Who loves the shining things of everyday:
> White curtain, and clean dishes, and swept floors,
> Where warm lights play,
> Who finds contentment in four lifted walls—
> I think that any man can safely take
> Such a woman to his heart to love
> For her own lovely sake.

We leave Grace Noll Crowell with two facts that belie her condition, whatever it was. She eventually received many awards, including the "Mother of America" award. And when Crowell hit her stride and presumably got up from her sick bed, her husband had to quit his newspaper job altogether to become her manager and accountant.

As the 20th century approached its halfway mark, the breadth of subjects widened for Texas poems. William Bard, Violette Newton, William Barney, and Vassar Miller come to mind for the variety of their subjects in their often intense evocative work.

From 1983 to the year 2000, there were no appointments made for the Texas Poet Laureate. It certainly was not for lack of candidates. The neglect was ameliorated by the appointment in 2000 of Dr. James Hoggard, an English professor at Midwestern State University in Wichita Falls, and a lively bunch of us has prevailed since.

In October of 2012, an historic gathering of Texas poets laureate occurred in Denton during the Ekphrastic Festival staged by the Greater Denton Arts Alliance. Six laureates read their poems one evening, all the poems on themes of the relationship between two arts, such as a poem which references a painting. Afterwards, in a cozy living room, they lifted a glass and exchanged stories of their tenures.

Dave Parsons of Conroe, the 2011 Poet Laureate, commented that he had a number of "requests to read poems at funerals for people I did not know from people that I did not know." He also related an offer of a bizarre business arrangement where he would lend his endorsement to a site where people would turn in haikus reviewing certain businesses.

James Hoggard, another poet laureate there that night, has pointed out that the correct pronunciation of the word "laureate" seems to elude even the most erudite. He has been introduced as the "law-ree-ETTE" on a number of occasions, as have I. I have wondered if that pronunciation was suggestive of a major-ETTE, and my evil twin immediately pictures myself prancing forth in white shiny boots and holding a baton.

Close by "law-ree-ETTE" is the pronunciation as "LAIR-ee-et." Now this is more in keeping with what a Texas poet laureate might be called. Get a rope!

Hoggard tells a wonderful story which illustrates the honor which seems to attach to the title. He had flown to Austin and back from Wichita Falls in a friend's private plane. "It was a hot August day, and when we got back, as I stepped off the plane, a man rushed up to the plane asking if he could have my keys, that he'd be glad to bring my car to the plane so I wouldn't have to get all hot and such, so I tossed him the keys, and off he ran in the afternoon heat and drove the car right up to the plane. Smiling, I kept thinking I could easily grow to like this. But that kind of thing didn't happen again."

Not even notoriety keeps away death, and in the described scene of the recent death of Mildred Baass of Victoria, the poet laureate from 1993 to 1995, we see the whimsy and grace of a poet. In an e-mail that went out from a fellow poet: "Those who knew Mildred will appreciate that she had a rosary in . . . [one] hand ... and a stuffed cat in the [other] hand."

My own poet laureate anecdotes include the fact that as I glanced over the long list from the *Texas Handbook*, a name chimed in my childhood memories. Ruth Reuther of Wichita Falls, the 1987-88 designee, was one of my mother's friends in Gainesville back in the 1940s. There are hardly ever six degrees of separation.

One of the most endearing things about being a poet laureate, besides the strange and often intoxicating reverence given to the post, is the fun that family, friends, and strangers have with the idea. Being crowned with laurel leaves, a la Olympia, is outlandish, flabbergasting, big enough in its sensationalism to be caught and exploited and appreciated by good Texans. My friends may tease me with a "Make way!" gesture. One had waiting for me when I arrived at her house a "crown" she had fashioned of a glittery Christmas tree drape.

When I go to my grandchildren's schools to speak in their classrooms, their toothy half-embarrassed smiles at their Jana being there, there in their very own classroom—even if I haven't brought cookies—is compensation enough for the wearying miles, paperwork, e-mails, and preparations.

I love it when a recalcitrant college student gives me the ultimate compliment: "I didn't know I was going to be able to understand your poems." And I don't mind having my picture made with someone's cousin or child. It's an honor to be honored, and such a request seems to me to be part of that mystique of being a proud Texan—both as the recipient of the request and as the requester.

Which gives me a way to end this piece, by telling a funny thing that happened to me on the way to my appointment. A little background: The Texas State Artists are four for each year: the 2-D Artist, the 3-D Artist, the State Musician, and the Poet Laureate. Since the Legislature only meets every two years, there are eight artists to be appointed in the ceremonies in the House of Representatives and the Senate.

On a beautiful May day in 2011, the eight of us were breakfasted in an Austin hotel and taken in a shuttle to the door of the Capitol, ushered in and told we'd need to be prepared to wait outside the chambers for the appropriate moment of our inductions.

Now the State Musician for 2011 was none other than Lyle Lovett. I got to visit with him quite a while in the ante-chamber, between folks coming up to ask for his autograph and photos with him. Afterward, the recipients reassembled on the steps of the Capitol for a final picture, and then were reunited with our families for further photo ops, hugs, and general merriment.

I was blessed to have my husband, three sons and their families and a number of friends there. Lyle Lovett graciously greeted some of them, and special note was made of his attention to my little grandsons, by now tugging at their ties. Of course, the cameras were clicking away.

Later in the week, my hometown paper, *The McAllen Monitor,* ran quite an extensive story on my selection. They took some of their photos from the Facebook pages of my grandsons' father's entries of the Austin celebration. They selected two pictures: a smallish head shot of me, and a large 5X5-inch one of Lyle Lovett greeting my grandsons.

Oh well, it was all in the family. Being a Texas poet laureate is the ultimate kinfolks experience.

Written for delivering in libraries, workshops and other public gatherings as a Scholar for the Texas Council on the Humanities, 2000+

Passing The Light: How Elder Wisdom Shapes the Future of Families

Several quick stories: What do they have in common?

1) A neighbor's grandchild came over to play in the yard. Mark was a beautiful fair child with light blue eyes and pale blond hair. When Mark fell and skinned his knee, he began to cry pitifully. I went over to inspect the damage. After Mark showed me the nearly invisible wound, he stopped crying, looked up at me with those gorgeous pale blue peepers, and said, "I'm really delicate, you know."

2) A father, when he takes his children on an outing, always gathers them first at the entrance of the park or building, and says, "If you get lost, come here and wait." Then he points out the green bench, the orange sign, the red pillars, or the fast food place just across the street.
"That's a good idea," another observes. The father stops. "I've never thought about it until now," he says, "but that's what we always did when we were kids."

3) Whenever a friend combs her hair, she says her mother's voice just at her shoulder murmurs, "You can't make a silk purse out of sow's ear." My friend says she's learned to say back, "Exactly what can be made out of sow's ear?" or, "But I never wanted to be a silk purse!"

4) Sara is six. At bedtime, she insists on cleaning the lint from between her toes. Her mother says, "That's your Aunt Nancy exactly—picky, picky, picky."

5) Diane, a woman of 50, comments on a friend's complaints about her housewife duties. "In my family," Diane says, "a woman's home duties are an honor, as well as a responsibility."

What do these stories have in common? They all show the power of family stories over us, even small stories— admonitions, observations, adages, comparisons, accusations, and compliments.

Russell Baker, in his award-winning autobiography *Growing Up*, writes:

> If my homework was done, I could sit with them and listen until ten o-clock struck . . . I loved the sense of family warmth that radiated through those long kitchen nights of talk . . . Usually I listened uncritically, for around that table, under the unshaded light bulb, I was receiving an education in the world and how to think about it. What I absorbed most deeply was not information but attitudes, ways of looking at the world that were to stay with me for many years.

The human being is a story-telling animal. Stories are basic to our survival. The telling of stories is one of the few things, besides the need for food, water, and shelter, that links us to our earliest predecessors. The bison and hunters drawn on the cave wall are evidence of early stories, as well as the breathtaking oral genealogies still evident in a few aboriginal cultures extant today.

Notice the difference in audience attention when the speaker is talking about abstract ideas and then launches into a story. If there's been coughing, looking around, indifference during the formal presentation of ideas, there is now rapt attention to the story.

Stories provide us with community. You tell your story; I gain something for my life from it. Hopefully, you gain from my stories. We see from our stories how we are similar and how we are different, and either way, we are brought closer for having been the teller or the listener.

We are always hungry for stories because we are trying to figure out our lives. Have others been in this situation? What, then, have they done about it? We are shaping ourselves as we live our lives, and we can never get too much information.

A certain kind of story has as its chief purpose to entertain, such as the mystery, or science fiction. But what of the stories told in our families? Certainly there are family stories told that have pure entertainment value, but family stories in particular are powerful and inordinately useful. They're instructive, and they teach, consciously or unconsciously the values, strengths, weaknesses, and expectations of those listening to them.

The family tale is not simply a past narrative, something over and done with, which happened to just anybody. It is in our human character to be "listening up," as it were, when we hear stories from our particular past. The things that happened to our ancestors, the way our ancestors were, what our grandparents tell us was the effect on them—all these things we are listening for, and they will go with us and reverberate throughout our lives.

If we hear a story of how our grandfather was a hot-tempered drunk, we may say, "So that's where I get my temper!" And if we are not alcoholics? Well, we simply haven't heard that part. We're listening to the parts of the story that confirm what we are looking out for.

Daniel Taylor writes in *The Healing Power of Stories*:

> . . . we are both chosen by and choose our stories. In our earliest years, our stories choose us. Later we have the ability and freedom to choose our stories. Some, of course, cling to us more tightly than others.

We are born bearing stories over which we have little control: how we were wanted or unwanted, how hard our birth was, what Uncle Ben said when he saw us. And we are added to the family lore. What we do in childhood becomes stories, all this, while we in turn begin to absorb the information presented to us that we may not even conceive of as "story," but simply as "the way things are," the things that are happening in our neighborhood, what our parents are complaining about or praising at the supper table, the daily rituals of eating, sleeping, working, interacting. These all come through the history of our families.

But as we grow, we begin to act as filters for the stories we hear. We reflect on what we have heard, and we start to develop the ability to choose the stories we like, those we want to be part of, and to reject or simply not hear those we dislike.

To illustrate: A writing student of mine told a family story she had learned only recently. It was a tragic tale of how her great-grandfather had shot and killed her great-grandmother. The woman died in the arms of her daughter. Ginger added at the end, "My grandmother [who was the daughter] was a good writer. She wrote all this down, describing it in detail with a lot of drama. My mother gave me the papers when I was home last time."

Ginger, the young talented writer in my class, might choose to remember the story for the fact that she had in her veins the blood of a murderer. Or, she could take from the story the fact that she is the descendant of a writer. She too might fulfill her dream of being a writer, partly because of the genetic boost.

From all this telling and hearing and interpreting of stories, we can take at least two implications:

> 1) We are living our lives out to a large degree by the formulae of our family stories; they shape us powerfully and always will;

> and

> 2) The stories we tell and the way we tell them can powerfully shape those who come after us.

It is this second fact: the stories we choose to tell and how we tell them that we want to take a closer look at.

The stories of our family's background and origin, their coming to America, their being here when others came, act as history lessons and guides to the nature of particular families.

Which boat did your family come on? The Mayflower? Captain Jones' slave vessel? A canoe down the St. Lawrence or up the Rio Grande?

How did they survive? Was it through skilled mercantilism, hard-scrabble farming, a fabulous stroke of luck, or sheer grit and determination?

What were their values?

Because I know my own family better than others, allow me to illustrate with my family. By the way, we of course come from many families. If we go back seven generations, we see we are drawn from 128 families! We usually take our cues about who we are from the families that we know most about. I'm talking here about my paternal grandfather's family and my maternal grandmother's.

My roots on both sides are Southern agrarian—not prosperous plantation owners but hardworking poor farming preachers and teachers. My father's people migrated from South Carolina to Arkansas—"because the country was sandy and could grow peaches" (that's always injected when the story is told)—and reached way back to Germany to name their little community in Arkansas "Bingen" after Bingen on the Rhine and yes, the home of the famous Hildegard of Bingen. My father is one of seven children, raised on a small-acreage farm. His father was a circuit-rider Landmark Baptist preacher on Sundays.

My mother's mother's family came from Mississippi and settled in English, Texas, up close to the Red River. My grandfather took his bride over into the Indian Territory and they lived and raised six children in a Native American community where my grandfather functioned for many years as the schoolmaster, the doctor, the moral instructor, and the interpreter of the law.

With that scanty background, would you be surprised at this list of what I perceive are family values I was raised with? Some of these I am proud of: I claim they have brought out my best self. Others, I am struggling mightily to change.

As I list these, ask yourself how you might agree or differ, and how you got the values you hold. Here are some of the attitudes and values I absorbed:

* Religious faith, with attendant church-going, should dominate everything else in life.
* Fear God. Love others whenever possible.
* Hard work will pay off.
* Divorce is a shameful thing.
* Women who smoke and men who drink are to be avoided.
* You help somebody if they're family, even if you don't like them.
* The rich will have a difficult time getting into heaven.
* The highest virtue is respectability.
* The most important thing in daily life is food—getting it, saving it, being thankful for it, preparing it, eating it all together as a family, and offering it to others as a token of hospitality.

Were these things drilled into me with conscious regularity? Certainly not. We simply practiced them, through word and deed—as it were. We waited until everyone was home to sit down to the supper table. We went to church, rain or shine. We took in the sick people in our family, or those who were down on their luck.

And I heard stories: How my maternal grandfather, when he was a teenager, was hired to deliver goods from town to other farm families living in his rural area and how, upon one occasion, he was charged to deliver some liquor to a neighbor. He wrote in his memoirs, "At every bridge, I stopped and sipped a little from the bottle, as an antidote to the poison of dangerous snakes lurking close by." The final lap of the trip resulted in his partner having to tie my poor adolescent grandfather across the horse and deliver him, limbs drunkenly flopping, to his own doorstep. Page two of the story: My grandfather never took on Demon Liquor again. The moral for all of us: Don't drink. The moral for my mother, keeper of family morals, as stated to a wayward brother: "Don't you know we can't drink? That our systems can't take alcohol? Don't you remember Daddy's story?"

Nearly every family origin story will contain a famous ancestor. In our family story, we are told that we are directly descended from William the Conqueror. I myself want to believe I am descended from Hildegard of Bingen, mentioned earlier, but I probably should abandon that myth since Hildegard was a pious nun.

My friend in the Valley, from eight generations of Hispanics living north of the Rio Grande, tells me he is directly descended from Cortez. In his case, he has impressive documentation to substantiate it.

Students in my autobiography classes volunteer famous ancestor stories right and left. "They say we're from the family of Marie Antoinette." "My great-great-great grandfather invented cricket." "Pancho Villa had several wives, you know, and who knows how many lovers. I'm from one of those relationships."

We love to claim kinship to presidents, kings and queens, notorious gangsters, inventors, and famous entertainers. Some kinship claims are perfectly valid. Others are based on less substantial evidence—the names are identical ["But my father's name is Grover Cleveland too"] or there's a trait to identify with ["I've got the Kennedy cowlick"]. In the case of my family, my female cousins and I, when we want to claim a little wildness, like to remember that Sally Rand, the famous burlesque entertainer, was our grandmother's second cousin.

We may smile as we think of these stories that connect our families with greatness of some sort, but the stories function usefully as well. They serve to tell our young, "You too can be great. After all, you inherited the same traits."

Family stories are so powerful that adopted children often adopt the history of their adopted family, no matter that there is no bloodline to follow. It's as if the spiritual and emotional bloodlines of adopted child and adopted family have been made manifest by the intentions of fate.

Sometimes wives know their husbands' family stories better than the husbands do. I often have women students in my writing classes who have enrolled in order to tell their husbands' family stories. This may be a natural talent of women, to be the story-keepers, the scrapbook makers, the connectors in the family. But it may also be a genetic predisposition by the mother to tie in to what is most interesting, relevant, strong in a family whose children are at least half of that clan.

One's family stories—though they may seem common and interchangeable with stories from other families—exert a huge influence on everyone in our particular family and our progeny. They serve to bind us together: "That's the McKinneys for you;" "You can't help it if you're a Bernbaum;" "We Gomezes don't do it that way." They give us a sense of belonging, however many warts and freckles our family has, and they make sure we huddle together and move forward. Family stories aid and abet the survival of the fittest. We have that instinctual urge to survive.

Parenthetically, that is why, on Christmas Day and the Fourth of July, we not only feel a great swelling of love in our hearts at family get-togethers for those clustered around the turkey or over the backyard smoker, but we are also willing to tolerate the company of loudmouths, drunkards, blowhards, neurotics of all sorts, near-do-wells, and possibly the worst, bores.

Another kind of origin story is the birthing story. What children are told about their births may powerfully influence their self-image. Elizabeth Stone, in her book titled *Black Sheep and Kissing Cousins* gives a very full discussion of the influence of birthing stories on the lives of those who are told the story of when they appeared in the world.

First-born males are often named after their fathers and grandfathers, so they have implanted early the suggestion that they will be like their male ancestors, perhaps in temperament, social standing, and profession. During the Middle Ages, when all commercial enterprise was a Mom-and-Pop operation, the adding of "& son," to the sign out front was a common, expected thing—and the son fulfilled his destiny of hat-maker, blacksmith, or tavern keeper.

In the past, males were more often told early on that they were "special" in some way as indicated by their birth. If the mother was in hard labor for 36 hours, the child was "special" by virtue of the pain. Conversely, if the child appeared in 20 minutes, start to finish, he might become "special" by virtue of the ease with which he made his worldly entry.

Human beings seem to crave ranking. In the past, parents were expected to choose a favorite, which child received the birthright. It was usually the eldest. The exception to the norm made history, for example, the ages-old Biblical story of the struggle between Isaac and Rebekah over which twin, Jacob or Esau, was "special" and thus entitled to Isaac's blessing and legacy.

All sorts of weather on the birthing day can be a portent served up to the little listener. "The sun was shining that day, and we knew we were blessed." One mother named her daughter "Stormy" because it *was* on the day she was born.

In Elizabeth Stone's research, she discovered something worth thinking about in relation to boys' or girls' births. Sons were told stories of being wanted, prayed for, special far more than daughters were. Of course, you will immediately think of the exceptions to this observation, as I did when I first read about it, but we're speaking of the result of surveys here, what seems to be the norm. Certainly there have always been parents who wholeheartedly wanted and got girls, those daughters being told stories of their specialness.

One of the peculiar things about the research is how often the stories of female infants and young girls being left in endangering situations came up, and, just as importantly, how these stories were told. Women told stories that their parents had told them of being left outside to "sun" in their prams and being forgotten for hours at a time, or being left in car seats overnight. The stories extended to how good little girls were to entertain themselves when they were sick, so much so that, if the illness was long-term, the caregiver might forget the child for hours on end.

In one story, Melinda, a toddler, wanders off naked and is found several houses away, picking flowers. This is not to say that many a young boy has not done the same. But it's interesting to note that this story, which has been told many times in family gatherings, is always related with light-hearted amusement, as though the danger inherent in such an escapade totally escapes the attention of the person telling the story. It is about the funniest thing that ever happened; neglect or a close call don't seem to have occurred to the parent.

Sally is told repeatedly that she was "blue, mangled, and had tremors every five minutes" when she was born. Additionally, her mother suffered long hours beforehand, and the doctor was drunk. What does Sally do with this information? Depending on how healthily she pulled out of her birth ordeal, she may come to believe—on her own—that she was meant to be, that she was God's gift to her parents and the world. On that premise she may move rapidly up the ladder of personal success, thankful she is alive and obviously one of the chosen. Or she may be guilt-ridden that she caused her mother so much distress, along with assigning every illness, every slight anomaly of her anatomy, to her poor entry into the world.

Stone writes:

Are girls left behind—forgotten in their carriages or car seats—more often than boys? The question is impossible to answer. But the fact is that girls, more often than boys, are told that they were forgotten and left behind.

Stone concludes that:

While not all sons report stories of sacred births and while not all daughters are told stories about births that have made their mothers sick, the fact is that sons alone participate in the aura of the sacred, and daughters alone do not.

Sometimes the message is mixed, and then the person has to decide which part he or she will believe. The story goes something like this:

Your birth almost killed me. But I've never regretted all the suffering and pain, the surgery afterward and the fact that I was so weakened. No, you have been worth every bit of the trouble and have made me proud every day of your life.

This is throwing out the baby with the bath of absolution.

A few birth stories seem to be the defining moment in the psyche of a person's life. Years ago, a student in an autobiography class wrote of her birth in a farm house on the Kansas prairie about 1930. Listen to her account:

> I was brought forth with instruments and handed to Grandma. "Put it aside; it won't live."
>
> Grandma didn't. She took charge of me. She stayed with us for days.
>
> The next day Dr. Whitson drove 24 miles to see Mother and noted, "It's still alive."
>
> Grandma asked for a formula.
>
> Dr. Whitson took her aside and said, "No, No, Mrs. Holt; it won't be here tomorrow."
>
> Grandma, determined I not die of starvation, soaked bread in water, dipped a clean cloth in this water and squeezed drop after drop into my mouth.
>
> The next day Dr. Whitson looked at me and shook his head. He gave Grandma a formula and medicine dropper. He cautioned everyone not to get their hopes up for if I did live, I probably wouldn't be "right."
>
> The instruments that saved Mother had left their mark on me. My head was misshapen, an ear nearly off, one eye almost out of the socket, the lid was torn on the other one. My mouth was pulled to one side, the top lip twisted, my jaw was crushed, and I was tongue-tied and couldn't cry. I had five deep gashes in my head. One arm was broken at the elbow.

There were other harrowing events in this young girl's life but she concludes, "By the grace of God I lived!" Can you imagine the bonding between the child and the grandmother, and how the story of her birth has informed her entire life? Every writing she did in the class after this initial one thanked God in astonishment and wonder for her existence.

In the present generation of children, a new means of telling the birth story has cropped up, the video of the birth itself. For

185

some, this means of commemorating the birth is as natural as baptism. One such technologically savvy family in San Antonio has ritualized the practice by showing the child his birth video on his birthday each year. The father, thinking about the implications of such a practice, commented, "Can you imagine what this might do to a child's psyche if he thinks he was born on television, a star, right up there with the other cartoon characters? And that the television gave him life?"

* * *

Now let's look at some family story motifs that may affect the young person and the adult. As we do, many of you will no doubt quickly call to mind the stories that have shaped your life.

Love:

Do you approve of falling in love at first sight, or will a love that is supposed to last forever be one that carefully grows from perhaps a modest friendship into a deepening appreciation for the traits of the beloved?

And then, does that love need a long courtship, or may the star-struck lovers immediately proceed to the justice of the peace?

The stories of love and marriage of the past will differ greatly with those of the future. One of the huge areas of behavioral change occurring in the 20th century has to do with love, marriage, childbearing, and divorce. The stories of circumspect courting, virgins at the altar, and vows of fidelity are often now heard and viewed as merely marvelous and quaint by young people today.

An older wife of my acquaintance, married some 60 years to her husband, told me recently of being approached at a family gathering by a carefree nephew who asked, "Aunt Beatrice, how long did you and Uncle Loyd live together before you were married?" In the telling of this incident, Aunt Beatrice is indignant. Her character and Uncle Loyd's are put to public scrutiny. In short, the question should never have been asked. "The very idea!"

To others within earshot, namely other cousins similar in age, the nephew's question was gauged all the way from "dumb and awful" to "he was just trying to make conversation so what did Aunt Beatrice get all excited about?"

"Relationships" have replaced "love affairs"; living together means something besides establishing a household after a marriage contract; and "serial monogamy"—if not openly acknowledged, may lie behind the altar vow and deep in the heart of a hesitant vow-taker.

In my family's history, poor as it was on all sides, it was the custom for young couples to live for about a year with one set of parents or the other. If it was with the husband's family, the young wife learned to make biscuits and fry chicken just the way her husband liked these delicacies. If the wife's, the bridegroom apprenticed to the business of his wife's father—learning blacksmithing or dairying or peanut farming. Thus, marrying was not strictly how and when one wanted to but involved the consent and blessing of entire families.

My maternal grandmother, to whom I was very close, gave me a great gift, the story of her courtship and wedding, which I recorded in a long poem about her life. That portion goes this way:

> I see her great astounding Victorian body—
> six-foot-tall bride with a sober hand
> resting on Grandfather's sitting-down shoulder.
> The wedding—a Sunday night after revival meeting,
> a trip 3 miles in a buggy home to her house,
> a sister going upstairs with her
> to help with a white nightgown,
> wide pink satin ribbon woven down the front,
> how she trembled when her sister left her
> at the top of the stairs,
> how she righted herself with a small smile
> when Grandpa, ascending, said,
> "Why Pearl, you look so pretty!"
> (She wouldn't tell me more.
> He had been dead fifteen years that afternoon.)

Divorce may be treated casually in one family and seriously in another. For young people still marrying—and the Sunday social pages show that the practice has not died away by a long shot—they may reflect on their families, perhaps even the example of their parents staying together—and be genuinely dismayed by the prospects of divorcing. Others agree that weddings are kind of fun, and if "things" don't work out, they'll not get too uptight about "splitting the blanket"—which term, they may or may not use, depending upon their family stories.

"First comes love, then comes marriage, then comes so-'n-so pushing a baby carriage!" Have you heard it lately? Will the girls in your family be learning it as a jump rope chant?

Of husbands and wives, one final observation: Whether whirlwind romances or carefully considered linkages of families, prospective husbands and wives would do well to share their family's stories. If "how it was in the old days" is vastly different between them, are they ready to accept living with a person with countering life tenets?

Money:

Importantly shaping some families are stories of fortune and money.

Did Uncle Minyard make his money honestly? If he didn't, is that the reason he lost it all? Why did our side of the family not enjoy the same affluence as the other? Was it plain bad luck, or bad judgment, or foolish living?

Stories of fortune, of money lost and money gained, lend themselves especially to the interpretation of the storyteller. If you are sitting at Cousin Alfa's dining table enjoying his fine meal, he may tell how he invested wisely and thus escaped some of the ravages of the Great Depression. On the other hand, if he is sitting at yours, and by the grace of your belief in the solidity of the family you have invited him to the best meal he'll have all year, he may still tell you how he escaped poverty during the Depression, but he'll be forced to say that it was the government that caused him to be reduced to his present circumstances.

The importance of money to a family is transmitted by storytelling, often the story just a quote from an ancestor. In my family, when there's been a house-burning or a robbery, we always quote my father's mother, a small pious twinkly woman whose hair was never cut in a lifetime. For losses that did not involve life itself, she would admonish, "Never mind. After all, it was only material."

This value functions very powerfully in our family framework. Recently, when one son reported theft of some of his things while attending a meeting in Cologne, Germany, and theft again in San Antonio the next day when he returned, I listened with amazement and chagrin, and after proper commiseration, found that I was saying to him, "I'm so glad you're safe. Think of the loss as strictly material."

He was kind enough not to say he did not have the stomach for his family's Anglo-Saxon Protestant cheeriness right then.

When it comes to family stories, everything depends more on the uses made of them than on their plots or consequences.

Politics:

Who was a staunch this or that in your family? And why? Did your family help elect the successful and popular leaders of the community and nation? Or did your ancestors show their freedom by organizing protests, supporting unpopular candidates and causes? Was there a renegade Democrat or Republican in the family, one who was ostracized from or beleaguered on family occasions?

Illness:

How do your family stories reflect attitudes toward illness? Have you been told so many times about your perilous childhood illnesses that you even now hesitate to join an exercise class? Do you stay on your feet, regardless of how you feel, because your grandfather milked the cows in wintertime even though he had influenza? Do you let your child stay home from school with a stomach ache, or do you remember that that was your ploy for skipping school and so take a tough approach to his infirmity?

Almost every family has one or two neurotic people who have made the stories of their health the focal point of their lives. Often these people live out their lives savoring the effects of a childhood illness or accident. And their healthy siblings may not forget the parental neglect resulting from the attention the sick child received.

Mental illness:

With its savage treatment in the past, it often lingers in the shadows of family stories. Taboo stories of sanitarium treatment, nervous breakdown, shock treatment, bizarre behavior— these stories, if they ever surface, often come as a surprise to a family. Nevertheless, they're important to know, in light of what has been discovered both about the hereditary nature of some of these mental disorders, and their ready detection and effective treatment through new means.

Sometimes suicide is a part of mental illness, but by no means always. Is there a family attitude toward suicide? That one should not consider it under any circumstances? That there is frequent instance of it? We have famous suicidal father-son pairs, such as Ernest Hemingway and his father; and Tennessee Williams and his father(?) but no one really knows whether the sons were genetically inclined, or if, in a dark hour, they were following the scripts of their forebears.

Contrast that with my friend Charles, whose brother committed suicide. Charles says, "Not me! Let him do with his life what he will. I'll not be imitating him." He is as adamant in self determination on the matter as others seem to be programmed.

Anger and violence:

What stories of anger and violence come from your family? Was anger expressed in verbal or physical abuse? Or was it by pouting, sarcasm, and coldness? Was your great-grandmother redheaded and temperamental? How was her hot temper handled—with great placation, or tit-for-tat in violent arguments in

190

the family? Did you children tiptoe around, seek out private hidey-holes to avoid the wrath of your mother or father? How were family arguments solved? These stories will in part determine how you handle anger. If you loathed your father's anger, you may have vowed not to be that way. If you idolized him, thinking he could do no wrong, you may feel your own explosive anger is justified in adulthood.

One of our family stories about anger comes directly from my husband's uncle. (Notice I say "our" family—owning my husband's as mine.) In the section of his memoirs about his late wife Mary Alice, Uncle Buddy writes:

> I used to have a very angry type of attitude and just fly off the handle at things. Well, she broke me of this because when I would have one of these, there would be sometimes two-three-four days that she wouldn't even speak to me, and I'd have to do a lot of apologizing. She finally calmed down the angry side of my life and it affected me greatly, which I'll never forget and appreciate always.

What a big man, to admit such! The story gives great comfort to a number of us in the family.

Race and racism:

Does your family lore contain stories of race or racism? More oppressed peoples will likely have more stories centering on race—stories that shore up the self-esteem of family members by touting the pre-imminent qualities of the race, as in the writing of Zora Neale Hurston, or by showing how family members were courageous in the face of racism. One of my students wrote on "What It's Like to Grow Up Mexican and Not Speaking Spanish"—a fact she has come to dislike.

A story about race can take whatever turn the teller desires it to take. For example, my friend Juan told a story about attending a relative's funeral in San Antonio, taking along his sister and aunt.

The deceased was of mixed parentage. At the meal following the funeral, the Anglos arrived first and clustered at one table while the Hispanics, of which Juan, his sister and aunt were a part, took the remaining table when they arrived. The Anglos did not seek to mingle with the out-of-towner Hispanics. My friend thought nothing of it, enjoying the company of those at his table, but he reported that his sister and aunt interpreted the seating arrangement as a racial slight and discussed it all the way home.

Gender image:

This subject is very important in many families and the stories often reflect what the family norms are. In one family, the script is written that by the boy's tenth birthday, he will have gone hunting or fishing with the men. Why? "Because we've always done it that way." In this particular family, when one of the grandchildren had his 13th birthday, and he expressed that he did not want to hunt game anymore, this was respected, but he was asked to and accepted to go along to the hunting camp with the other males, just for the ride.

As courtship, marriage, and child-raising traditions have been upended in the last few decades, so has the rigidity of sexual roles in families. This is no doubt due to the facts that our work is not muscle-based anymore, that the women's movement was a source of enlightenment about gender equality, and that there has been a great deal of social and biological investigation into the nature of human sexual preference.

For those who feel that our world is on the brink of dissolution because of the prevalence of gay and lesbian activity, perhaps they should look to their own family stories, where homosexuals existed gamely under such genteel names as "gay bachelors," "maiden ladies," "old maids," "dandies," and "fops." Maybe it is not that we have more homosexuals now, but that our family stories have quit hiding, either by taboo, or semantically, their normal presence in the population. Are the gays in your family appreciated for their contributions to society, or do your stories seek to ostracize them? What is the message of your family to the world and to them about tolerance, playing the hand one was dealt, and self-worth?

* * *

Perhaps this discussion has made you aware of some of your family's stories and how these generate life and energy, awareness and values to new members. I want to talk some now about the role elders in the family can play in telling their stories.

Daniel Taylor, in *The Healing Power Of Stories,* observes that "Middle age makes storytellers of us all." While we are alive, Taylor says, we have the opportunity be both the characters in the stories and the co-creators. "There is an ongoing tension between living as our stories dictate as opposed to dictating the stories we live. We both shape and are shaped by stories."

Thus, when I speak now of elders, I'm talking to those of us who are middle-aged and past. Most cultures have valued the wisdom of the mature. In pre-writing cultures, it was the job of the old people to recite the history of a people, from their creation on down, to the young. And the young were required to pay close attention. An African proverb says: "When a knowledgeable old person dies, a whole library disappears."

Some of the reverence for the stories of elders has been lost in our modern age. The emphasis on the top-dollar value of youth and their money, a technology of speed, the institutionalizing of education, an increase in the mobility of families—all these have contributed to the neglect of old people and their stories.

Gratefully, there has been in the last 20 years or so, a revival of interest in memoirs, in writing autobiographies, and lately, in diversifying from the written page into storytelling on audio and video tapes. Now thousands of older people are writing their memoirs, many at the request of their children. I teach autobiographical writing because other people's lives interest me a great deal, and I believe in the power of family stories to transform the lives of both tellers and listeners.

Stories from the old have value because elders have lived through so much. Their ways have been tried and found true. Or tried, and found wanting, with the consequences. The old are eager to tell their stories. In every age there have been remarkable stories from the old, but I think the stories of our old today are particularly interesting and needful because of the fantastic changes that have taken place during the past century, the time of their lives.

Robert Akeret, in his book *Family Tales, Family Wisdom,* observes:

> When elders tell their stories to families, it is a renewal for all: Children see their parents in a new light—an individual with a life and subjectivity of their own; there is renewed respect for elders and a deeper understanding of themselves . . . They tell, ultimately how all of those listening fit into the life cycle. They provide maps of ways to live.

There are many different ways to tell one's stories. As an elder, you can make some choices about the methods. Almost always, it is a mixture of methods. Of course, the formal method is to write it all down. If you can write a comprehensive autobiography of about 200 typewritten pages, you can leave your family a significant gift. Many people are doing just that, and they are feeling great reward and personal satisfaction and discovery from reviewing their lives in this way.

But maybe writing a book sounds like a daunting task to you. Then begin to write a few good stories down, simply as they occur to you. And you needn't confine it to "stories" per se, with beginnings, middles, and endings, composed in perfectly developed paragraphs.

Write down family sayings: admonitions, observations, charges, warnings, teasings, rules. The other day I asked my creative writing class for some sayings from their families, and in a matter of minutes, they came up with:

"Men don't cry,"

"You eat too fast,"

"Finish it—it's just a dab,"

"Some people are so good that they're good for nothing,"

"If you're going to do something, do it right the first time," and

"God helps those who help themselves."

Write down recipes, including notations such as "I made this coconut cake for Sam's birthday each year." Write down directions for the crafts you practice and the work you do. Tell the secrets of growing hybrid lilies or skinning a squirrel. Photocopy the pattern of quilt square you are famous for. Tell step by step how you go about refinishing furniture or catching fish. Draw floor plans of a house in your childhood. Once in class I got a beautiful barn floor plan, along with commentary from a memoir writer. Don't forget maps of the little town where you lived.

Sample grocery lists, to-do lists, bills of lading, certificates of all kinds. Favorite Bible verses and poems and passages from literature. Lists of favorites: songs, colors, trees, flowers, people, and places. Lists of your major travels and lists of famous people you have met or seen. Letters—sometimes with your explanation of the subject, as well as telegrams, school papers, and report cards.

These are all components of your autobiography and may serve as a record of your life, even though the information they transmit is not in well-ordered paragraphs. A journal kept faithfully but not necessarily daily through the years is a precious keepsake for your family. A friend showed me recently her mother's five-line diary, kept up to date for 40 years. It made fascinating reading.

Denise Linn in her book *Sacred Legacies* suggests that you write a "legacy story" rather than or in addition to your autobiography. The legacy story is a gift to your heirs. In your legacy story, you might consciously choose a theme: Let's say, "The Great Spirit is looking out for me in everything that has happened in my life." In details, you would show how this was borne out in your life. You might choose both bad-at-the-time and wonderful-at-the-time events, but they would all eventually show that yes, in everything, the Universe (read "God" or "fate" or whatever) was guiding you through. Whether you will edit your life to include only the good, bold, and beautiful things, or you feel your life has been a cautionary tale and you want your autobiography to show your children how not to live—these things are up to you.

As Daniel Taylor says, "Depending on how skeptical one is, stories either reveal the underlying connectedness of things or give us the illusion of connectedness in a random world."

But a legacy story is different from an autobiography in that you are thinking always: "What from my life do I want to tell those who come after me that will help them in their living?" You may tell all, very little, or select out some things that were especially meaningful or painful for you while choosing to keep other things private.

As an aside, we need to examine carefully the stories of our lives that we have been withholding. For example, what is so shameful about having immigrated to this country that we never speak of it? Should we not tell that story, especially if it illustrates history and shows courage and betterment of lives of those involved?

Of the horrendous experiences of war, some have chosen not to ever speak. It may be that their war was unpopular, or when they tried to speak of it, they were teased about "telling old war stories." But shouldn't the stories of sacrifice, struggle, victory, and defeat be shared with those who enjoy the benefits of freedom? Or, on a darker note, don't we need witnesses to the madness of war as a human activity?

If you have never told a certain event out of your life, could it be because you have been mistakenly assuming someone would not be interested. My late mother-in-law was one of the most modest people I have ever known. She told me two stories from her life—quite by accident and after I'd been in the family for many years—that were fantastic in their significance for social and cultural history.

One evening we were talking about hair, and Nannah said, "Did I ever tell you about the time I went riding with my beau?" It seems the ride was taken in the open cockpit of a bi-plane which her sweetie was piloting. They flew around one Sunday afternoon

196

and when they returned she found that her hair was an incredibly tangled mess. She laughed, "It took me nearly a week to get my hair unscrambled."

Her other story came after her casual statement that as a child, she first learned to read backwards. Why was this? She said:

> Well, you know we were in vaudeville, and when the silents came in, we were not the main act but were booked to play tunes while they changed reels. So we sat backstage, behind the screen, while the movie was projected. We read the captions through the screen, from behind, and of course the words appeared backwards. so that's how I learned to read.

Astonishing! Why had she never told us that? Well, she hadn't really thought anyone would be interested!

So, look at all your life, even the parts you thought were too embarrassing, or horrendous, or uninteresting to tell, and see if some of those things would be worthwhile to share.

And remember that no one ever said our life stories had to be sworn to in court as the truth, the whole truth, and nothing but the truth. It is your choice. The only bad choice is in choosing not to share anything at all of yourself.

But suppose you have no one asking you to write your stories. Perhaps your children are far away, geographically or in spirit. You may even have experienced a "discouraging word" as the song "Home on the Range" says. Is it worth it to write your life story?

I say yes, because if you have heirs, or nieces and nephews, or live in a community where there will be children born, there will almost certainly be some person from your family line or larger community clan as yet unborn who will yearn for your stories. You do not know this person yet. She is still a star; he is a twinkle in the eye of God. But I can assure you, from many, many conversations with those stars and twinkles which have become people, that your story will be appreciated.

Now I want to say a word to the mid-lifers and young people in the families of the old. Sometimes it is hard to sit still for the stories of the old. Until the present revival, elder stories have not been much in fashion in our nation.

James Hillman, the noted author of *The Force Of Character And The Lasting Life,* puts it this way:

We don't realize the practical value of older people. We attribute to old age wisdom and sagacity and all these good things, but we don't have much use for that in our get-up-and-go culture . . . old people are very practical for society: they know a lot; they've acquired many skills ... We need to look at old people more practically in order to restore their value.

Parents of teenagers and young adults, it is imperative that you be the leaders in guiding your young adults to take time to hear the stories of the old people in your family. Insist that teenagers go on family outings. Remind your adult children who are in the busiest times in their working lives that their grandparents must be held in their hearts and minds, and that visits to them should be worked into their busy lives. Almost without exception, they will bless you, if not presently, at least later, for your words of encouragement.

"But," they may say, "Aunt Matilda is difficult, quarrelsome, boring." Urge them to go anyway, and challenge them to sidetrack Aunt Matilda—from her litany of bodily pain and perhaps the bad food she's being served, sidetrack her to tell stories of her life. Foraging beyond the difficult personality traits with some magnanimous patience can be a mighty lesson in maturity for our young people.

"But Uncle Ben tells the same old stories over and over," your children say. Challenge them to listen for new material, to examine how the story changes from one occasion to the next. Remind them that the story is being told repeatedly because, among other things, it obviously was very important in the life of the storyteller.

I recently taught autobiographical writing at a national conference center in the Southwest. An 85-year-old woman came across the country from New Jersey with a plan to join a certain session of the conference. When she arrived, she found to her dismay that it met halfway up a mountainside. Unable to navigate the steep climb, she was reassigned to my group, which met on the level plain.

The first day Clara emphasized that she was not interested in writing her memoirs, since she had no one to pass them on to.

But in the course of the week, she managed to participate in the assignments, still remaining somewhat to herself and a bit acerbic about the writings of others in the class.

On the last day, she brought to class a writing about going on a picnic in India when she was a child, and how they had to take a servant along especially to watch for tigers. She had managed to keep hidden for a whole week her fascinating childhood in India as the daughter of missionaries. Class members, who had struggled through the week in kindness to help this old person make the best of her week, were enthralled by her account. Afterward, a man whom she'd been particularly critical of during the week, "because you don't enunciate correctly—you need to open your mouth more"—this man went warmly to her side and they began animated talk about living in Bombay.

I recently received a letter from Clara. This is what she wrote:

> As you are wondering what we are doing about using the incentive you gave us in class, be assured that I am. I've written almost thirty typewritten pages already, and am having a lot of fun doing it!

And about the class, she commented,"We really almost seemed like a family, didn't we?"

* * *

In conclusion, let us not forget a few key things:
We all, at any age, pass the light to generations to come. Teenagers can take time to tell appropriate stories from their lives to small fry. Anybody around can and should tell bedtime stories, supper table stories, stories on walks, on front porches, around Christmas trees. Let's not let the great technological mouth tell all our stories. It isn't the same.

Eudora Welty wrote in 1984:

Long before I wrote stories, I listened for stories. Listening for them is something more acute than listening to them. I suppose it's an early form of participation in what goes on. Listening children know stories are there. When their elders sit and begin, children are just waiting and hoping for one to come out, like a mouse from its hole.

In telling your life story, remember that the past, as well as the future, is malleable. Your interpretation of what happened in your life will be changing as long as you live. From time to time, re-examine your stories. Do you see an event in a different light now? Has a new meaning occurred to you? Do you have new information?

A student in one of my classes wrote about a time when she and her new husband were saying goodbye to his parents so that her husband could report for active duty in WWII. At the time, the young bride and her mother-in-law were on chilly terms. As they said goodbye, the older woman's mouth twisted in a bitter shape, and for years, the daughter-in-law assumed the facial gesture was a goodbye smirk at her. Only recently had she come to the realization that the older woman's face was contorted in grief and love for her son who might never return. Be aware that your interpretations of your past are always changing, and may be changed in your accounts as well.

Telling our stories and allowing others to tell theirs may heal us. Our stories connect us with others: we share and feel ourselves a part of the ancient circle around the campfire.

Without our stories, we are patternless. The world needs our stories to remind them of values and choices, to explain experience, to show wonder, the power of free will, and, as Joseph Campbell put it, simply "the rapture of being alive."

We achieve a kind of balance when we tell our stories and when we receive those of others. By articulating in words the events, thoughts, actions, meditations, interpretations of our pasts, we come to understand our present, and we benefit the future of those we love.

The Kiowa writer Scott Momaday tells of being taken as a small boy by his father to visit his great-grandmother. She took Scott's hands in hers and wept softly as she pronounced her blessing on him. Momaday writes of the incident:

> That was a wonderful and beautiful thing that happened in my life. There, on that warm, distant afternoon: an old woman and a child, holding hands across the generations. There is great good in such a remembrance; I cannot imagine that it might have been lost upon me.

So let us pass the light, not the darkness, by telling our stories often and well. Let us trust that our stories will fall on ears that can take them and shape them for the goodness of life and for the ongoing of our spirits.

Let us tell our stories with truth, grace, joy, and hope.

Part Six: Poems About Writing

There is a pleasure in poetic pains which only poets know.
~William Cowper

Stretch

If a poem is a field
with row on row of words,
some already gone to seed
when you visit of a morning,
some in a low place yellowed
with clichés of water or salt,
others ravaged by a local plague—
already said, thought, farmed out—
Still, there may be a ripeness,
a harvest waiting, plump and full,
rows you lift high your legs for,
stepping across full bolls
or red juice in a ball, or hidden roots,
or the dashes of beans against a
blackbirded sorghum.
Though a jackrabbit startles,
there's weevil and borer evidence,
and you knew right off one oughtn't
to try walking a field this big,
the sun bearing down,
any number of snakes,
stride too short for the
beckoning rhythm of the lines.
Still, you did it, you did it,
and finally you're standing,
looking back, hands on hips,
in this southeast corner of the poem.

Riff

At the neck of the word,
the tube that gets no respect,
at the neck of the word,
no, not entirely the head,
with its careful round thoughts,
its cerebral priss,
nor yet in the body,
a nonsense of sounds—
awful palpitations
and twitchings,
ague and gut growl—
not that either,
but at the neck of the word,
where brain and gut meet,
where meaning and moaning
smooth together,
conjoin,
form a tunnel
piping what
we're trying to say—
Hallow! We call—
Hallow! It's dark in here
in here
at the neck of the word.
On the verge of
the truest thing
we've ever spoken
and the chopping block:
this place,
the neck of the word.

My Big Chief Tablet Is Trying to Speak
at the Writers' Retreat

So far, this new yellow writing tablet,
beckoning as a daffodil,
smooth as a dog's tongue,
patient to the day of judgment,
sunshine with sky blue lines,
drug of choice to the pen,
safe haven for homeless words
has
lined a rain-soaked deck chair,
stanched a leak in the cabin ceiling,
received a berry deposit from a bird,
tendered a sign: *Squirrel Loose in Bathroom,*
saved the environment from gum,
collected this list.

Samuel Taylor Coleridge, I Hear You

At this moment he was unfortunately called out by a person on business from Porlock, and detained by him above an hour, and on his return to his room, found, to his no small surprise and mortification . . . all the rest had passed away.

—Preface to "Kubla Khan"

I got out of bed in the dark
with the most moist poem
I had ever thought.
It felt right.
It smelled right
and was holding still.
I turned on the light
because obviously,
I said,
I can't see the lines
unless there's light.
I found a pencil.
The thing immediately
jumped down,
crawled under the bed
and refused to come out.
All night it made
obscene lumps
in my mattress.

Ovulation

An idea late last night
drifted toward the heart
sent pulsing signals
gave a slight fever
and made her desiring.

Finding nothing in the way
to couple with and bloom
nor any staying powers
it gave up. Next morning
it left by way of a schedule.

Things I Did Not Say at a Junior High
Poetry Workshop

Any other way is better to get loved.
Gargle with the following:
      "Relationships are more important than poems.
       Poems are more important than relationships."
Whichever gags you, abide by the other.

A poem is not a 40-hour week,
is better than sleeping pills,
is equivalent to a burp or dandruff
at rodeos, beauty salons, grocery stores,
family reunions.

A poem, read in the afternoon among furs,
will have the little foxes crying real tears;
if coddled, may run into the bushes,
may lie down grinning and dead as a possum.

Poems have been known to hide in songs
and toilet compartments,
can become mouthfuls of lozenges.

Sometimes a poem burns the eyes
like a solar eclipse, blinds the poet.
Look to the sense of it
through smoked lens.

Including the above,
all generalizations about poems
are false.

Lecturing on Sylvia Plath

After her villanelle "Mad Girl's Love Song"

I shut my eyes and all the class drops dead;
I lift my lids and there they are again.
(I wish I'd made them up inside my head.)

I try to make them see that what she said
and what she did were not summarily insane.
I shut my eyes and all the class drops dead.

They drum their pens at babies pickled, tulips red,
list 3 important points on Esther's pain.
(I wish I'd made them up inside my head.)

The boys stretch and see themselves in bed
with girls who haven't poems on the brain.
I shut my eyes and all the class drops dead.

Studying sickies—you sure can't get ahead;
lots of women with kids don't complain.
(I wish I'd made them up inside my head.)

Black stars and rooks and bell jars are too sad.
Poets are nuts. To kill yourself is sin.
I shut my eyes and all the class drops dead.
(I wish I'd made them up inside my head.)

An Open Letter to Composition Students

Strive to make your writing unified, coherent, and complete.
—composition manual

Today we are talking of compound sentences;
tomorrow, the paragraph; next week, the essay.
Sometime I will ask you for papers.
Sometime I will walk between the rows
collecting your writing. You will fold the paper
and write your name on the front.
You will toss it to me, or schmooze it to me,
or put it in the wrong stack on my desk.

We reach an uneasy peace about comma splices,
assignments for tomorrow, the objective case,
the thesis sentence. You stay bound in your notes.
I stay clipped in my grade book.
You hand in bits of yourself.
I pass back minims of myself.
You need to hate me a little
because it is something students do.
I need to hate you a little
because it is something teachers do.

But someday after I post your final grade
and you see it, grab your temples and swear,
or grab your friend and leap like a glad fool
there in the narrow hall, someday later we may meet
on a covered walkway between classes.
Do not be surprised if I comma your elbows
lightly with my hands, my former student
with thick hair and white teeth,
in jeans and sloganed T-shirt. Do not be surprised
if I tell you, there on the covered walkway,
without my grade book and in less than 500 words,
that you are unified, coherent, and complete.

Directions for Writer's Vacuum

Sneak up on the words—
loops, dots, posts, curls inside the page.
Drag them cowering out of the whiteness,
line on line. Find them out,
plunder them with the pen or pixel,
tickle them until they scream
themselves literate,
high contrast on the page.
Know whatever's white hides the truth.
Whatever's blank harbors words
longing to be colored in,
their jots and tittles connected.

Self-help Manual

I. Confessional poets

Grasp the front flaps of yourself firmly
Wait for a group of people laughing and unconcerned
Leap out with a samurai cry, planting your feet wide
Show every part that's been giving you trouble
Do not think of the future

II. Lyric poets

Announce a weekend retreat devoted to trancing
Lay in a supply of sangria and gum
Retrieve CDs from friends
Make a smoky bonfire of punctuation and syntax
Say prayers to Saint Joyce and Saint Hopkins
Fall in love with your voice box

III. Mood poets

Awake mindless
Brew a cup of anything
Discover leftovers of an old love affair under bed
Stare out the window at birds, grass, trees
Begin the poem "Today, I must write a poem"
End the poem "I know not why the rain falls."

Dear Esteemed Writer

Every year we get thousands of submissions,
of which yours of course was only one.
It has been read by our advisory board.
Note that we are thanking you upfront for it.
But your work is just not quite right for us.

Now for the truth:
Your bio lacks the term "award-winning" in it.
No one has called you "amazing" or "awesome."
Your "Likes" on Facebook are slim.
You do not have videos on YouTube.
We could not find your blog.
(We texted you for a better link
but received no reply.)
In fact, your rap is an old shawl.
Your groove is deep as a rut.
Your mojo has moseyed off.
Your work does not show
a sad childhood, a murderous sibling,
or even an explicit word picture of sex
or a neighbor smoking pot.
Finally, we were very disappointed that
your bio does not mention that you live
with two wonderful cats, a parrot,
and three donkeys in a wilderness.
Still, we wish you the best.
Above all, keep writing!

The Critic Helps the Poet

The first 3 lines of this poem
are too prosaic. The second
sentence jerks—tone changes.

DO NOT READ THE ABOVE.

Lines 4-7 show some development
of the idée fixe but
wander too much—thus
chatty and indulgent.

STRIKE lls. 4-7.

Any images coming up are
1) self-serving
2) too easy
3) mannered
4) trivial
5) creaking
6) offensive to my taste.

OMIT ALL QUALIFYING 1) THROUGH 6).

The ending is lame and inept,
sentimental and uncontrolled.

DO NOT END THIS POEM.

P.S. It's a marvelous poem
(tho' not terribly ambitious).

Bookmark

Thank you for waiting patiently until we return,
red lace of Switzerland, green leather of Ireland,
papier mâché with sloe-eyed natives harvesting.
Still, you have a life of your own, a job to envy.

Who would not like, hour after hour, to be pressed
with ideas in the den, feel the tickle of feathers
from a coffee table hawk, be allowed to snigger
at a bathroom cousin shut in an academic journal?

Plastic Pharaoh new-dug from the museum store,
embroidered red poppy of an August birthday,
laminated rosemary from a Northwest garden,
tiny zarape migrating from the Mexican market,

placemat laid for a dinner of paragraphs,
rooster crowing from the edge of the page,
prisoner condemned to the medieval press
or a long, long wait on the chopping block,

transformed from souvenir to consort
of the best words in their best order,
what's it like to hold a place in time and space,
to separate yesterday from tomorrow?

And what's not to envy in your life—
to be lifted with love, fingered, nibbled, held close,
and, when all is known for now,
put back between the sheets?

Book Learning

How can we ever know
what the words do
when we close a book?
Perhaps p. 38 swamps 37,
the end of chapter 10
sniffs the epigraph of 11,
thick paragraphs on 142
insist on street-dancing.

The dialog on 213 may go
for treatment of hiccups.
Could it be
that charts switch facts,
photos pick fights
with their captions?

Things could get serious;
"Index" offends "Contents,"
Margins surge type,
titles intermarry.

If only bookmarks would
share their voyeur rights,
if words would quit acting
like falling trees
in earless forests,
like fridge lights after
the mayo is retrieved.

Until then, we may never know
what the words really say.

This Poem, Waiting

This poem waits like a dog on a porch,
like a baby waking, like a rapist in an alley.

The poem squirms when I touch it,
wrinkles its nose at my chosen words.

It acts out when approached by rhythm,
leaves a suicide note but is only running away.

The poem makes me smile when I waken,
knows I want it in the worst way.

It lolls, writing my name in calligraphy,
hates me for being jealous of its beauty.

The poem knows its kind is overpopulating,
should be practical, get a job, get a life.

But it begs to win prizes, fellowships,
be fine-bound like its New York cousins.

This poem is thirsty, prayerful, and snotty.
It inverts, glows, blacks out.

It jumps out of a closet, off the high board,
from the 49th floor, skydives in New Mexico.

It is dying for the perfect close, for saying,
in an utterly original way *The End*.

References

Some of these notations are for references to articles, stories, and poems first published in a periodical or in one of the author's books. Many works were republished by other publications. Other citations here reference writers mentioned in articles and presentations.

Airlift. Lamar University Literary Press, 1992, "A Private Miracle."
Robert Akeret. *Family Tales, Family Wisdom,* William Morrow, 1991.
Ampersand 20, "Riff,""Bookmark."
Ancient Cud, 1977, "The Critic Helps the Poet."
Sherwood Anderson. "Death in the Woods," *Death in the Woods and Other Stories*, Boni and Liveright, 1933.
Appearances. Lamar University Literary Press, 2012.
Carlos Ashley. *That Spotted Sow & Other Hill Country Ballads,* Shoal Creek Publishers, 1975.
Russell Baker. *Growing Up*, Congdon & Weed, 1982.
Blue Mesa Review, 1998, "Big Bird Inhabits Rio Grande Valley in 1976."
Bonds, riverSedge Press, 1978, "Ovulation."
Both Sides of the Border. Texas Folklore Society LXI, 2004. "Passing the Light: How Elderwisdom Shapes the Future of Families" published as "Passing the Light: How Family Stories Shape Our Lives."
CCTE Proceedings 1981, "McCully's Sod House."
Coe Review, 1996, "How the Neighbors We Never Meet . . ."
Concho River Review, 2014, "Tripping the Light Fantastic."
Marshall Cook, University of Wisconsin creative writing program newsletter.
Eclectica, 2009, "Stretch."
English in Texas, 2014, "Creative Joy: Process and Product."
E.M. Forster. *Aspects of the Novel,* Edward Arnold, 1927.
Goodbye, Mexico. "Transfiguration," Texas Review Press, 2015.
Gray Sky Review, II, "One More for Sylvia."
James Hillman. *The Force of Character and the Lasting Life,* Random, 1999.
Isosceles, 1997, "After Sunday."

Journal of English Teaching Techniques, 1976, "An Open Letter to
     Composition Students."
Langdon Review of the Arts, 2012-13: "Why I Write,""Directions
     for Writer's Vacuum,""Dear Esteemed Writer," and 2004,
     "Preface to Poems."
Latitude 30°18', 1985, "Self-help Manual."
Denise Linn. *Sacred Legacies,* Rider & Co, 1999.
The Mesquite Review, 1998, "Confessions of a Genre Jumper";
     1997, "A Private Miracle"; 1999, "My Big Chief . . . ."
Scott Momaday. *The Names: A Memoir,* Harper, 1976.
Howard Moss. *The Poet's Story,* McMillan Co, 1973.
The Nuts-and-Bolts Guide to Writing Your Life Story. The
     Knowing Press, 1998, "The Hang-up Nobody Talks About."
Ordinary Charms. Lamar University Literary Press, 2017.
Grace Paley. "Conversations with Grace Paley," *The American
     Audio Prose Library,* 1986.
The Pikestaff Forum, 1978, "Things I Did Not Say . . ."
Beatrice Plumb. *Grace Noll Crowell: The Poet and the Woman,*
     Harper and Bros., 1938.
riverSedge, 1977, co-founder's statement; 1978,"Samuel Taylor
     Coleridge, I Hear You"; 1994, "After Long Silence"; 2014,
     Introduction.
Roundup: an Anthology of Texas Poets, Prickly Pear Press, 1999.
"Santos and the Tree Warriors," *The Valley,* riverSedge press, 1979.
Scribe, Writer's League of Texas, vol. 27, "Institutionalize
     Yourself."
Start Writing Now, 2004, "Craft a Welcoming Title."
Elizabeth Stone. *Black Sheep and Kissing Cousins*, Transaction
     Publishers, 2004.
The Story Circle Network Journal, 2002, Interview.
Story Magazine, n.d. Sara Burnaby, "Bears."
"Take Cover," *RE:AL,* 1998.
Tarleton State University, *Anthology 19,* Creative Arts Day, 2013.
Daniel Taylor. *The Healing Power of Stories,* Doubleday, 1996.
The Texas Observer, "Book Learning," 2009.
The Texas Review, "This Poem, Waiting," 2011.

Texas Weather, Lamar University Literary Press, 2016, "A Private
    Miracle."

The Valley, riverSedge press, 1979.

The Village Advocate, 1988.

Eudora Welty. *One Writer's Beginnings*, Harvard University Press,
    1984.

The Wonder Is, 2nd edition, Ink Brush Press, 2012.

Writer's Digest, May 2003, "Craft a Title That Beckons."

About the Author

This miscellany comes out of a long career in writing and teaching by Jan Seale. Educated at Baylor University, the University of Louisville and the University of North Texas, she lives in the subtropical Rio Grande Valley of Texas.

In addition to the twenty-seven books in various genres she has authored, her writing has been published in such venues as *Texas Monthly, Writer's Digest, Newsday, The San Francisco Chronicle*, and *The Yale Review*. Two of Seale's stories have been presented on National Public Radio and four plays have received performances.

Seale is the 2012 Texas Poet Laureate. She has held a National Endowment for the Arts Fellowship and has been a Humanities Scholar for Humanities Texas, as well as an Artist-in-the-Schools for the Texas Commission on the Arts. She holds membership in the Texas Institute of Letters.

Seale has three sons and four grandsons.

www.ingramcontent.com/pod-product-compliance
Lightning Source LLC
Chambersburg PA
CBHW030825090426
42737CB00009B/872